T0247587

KGB MAN

*The Cold War's
Most Notorious
Soviet Agent
and the First to
be Exchanged
at the
Bridge of Spies*

CECIL KUHNE

A KNOX PRESS BOOK
An Imprint of Permuted Press

KGB Man:
The Cold War's Most Notorious Soviet Agent and the First to be Exchanged
at the Bridge of Spies
© 2023 by Cecil Kuhne
All Rights Reserved

ISBN: 978-1-63758-592-4
ISBN (eBook): 978-1-63758-593-1

Interior design and composition by Greg Johnson, Textbook Perfect

Permuted Press, LLC
New York • Nashville
permutedpress.com

Published in the United States of America
1 2 3 4 5 6 7 8 9 10

"One of the basic precepts of secret intelligence is that nothing should ever be done simply if there are devious ways of doing it."

—MALCOLM MUGGERIDGE

CONTENTS

BRIEF TIMELINE OF EVENTS

1948 Rudolf Abel, with cryptonym of "Mark" and aliases of "Andre Kayotis," "Emil Robert Goldfus," and "Martin Collins," illegally enters US through Canada

October 21, 1952 Reino Häyhänen, with cryptonym of "Vic" and alias of "Eugene Nicolai Maki," illegally enters US through New York City

Summer 1954 Abel and Häyhänen meet in person

Fall 1954 Abel and Häyhänen given instructions from Moscow to locate Roy Rhodes, with cryptonym of "Quebec," an American serving as a KGB agent

June 10, 1955 Abel travels to Russia on KGB business

Summer 1956 Abel arranges for Häyhänen to return to Russia on leave

April 24, 1957 Häyhänen leaves for Russia

May 1957 Häyhänen defects to American Embassy in Paris

June 21, 1957 Abel arrested

November 19, 1957 Abel convicted of espionage and sentenced to thirty years in prison

PROLOGUE

Early in May of 1957, a burly, mustachioed thirty-six-year-old Soviet spy from Finland named Reino Häyhänen walked briskly down *l'avenue Gabriel*, the famed tree-lined boulevard in Paris. Wearing large, dark sunglasses and a felt fedora pulled tightly over his head to conceal his identity, Häyhänen sharply turned the corner and shoved open the large, wooden doors leading into the grand hall of the American Embassy. He marched inside, his heels clicking briskly on the expensive marble tiles.

Häyhänen asked to see the ambassador, announcing to those assembled around him that for the past five years he had been a KGB operative working in the United States. The embassy staff ushered Häyhänen in, told him to have a seat, and then asked to see his identification papers. Häyhänen reached into his coat pocket and pulled out a fake US passport that bore the name of "Eugene Nicolai Maki."

For the next several hours, Häyhänen confessed that, while he was in the States, he transmitted sensitive US military data to Moscow. He engaged in the typical espionage activities—making chalk marks in Central Park to indicate that secret messages were ready for pickup, leaving tiny microfilm in hollowed-out coins, picking up bundles of cash at a lamppost hideaway, and standing in a subway station wearing a red-striped tie and smoking a pipe to identify himself to another spy. After the embassy personnel had gathered a dossier beyond their wildest dreams, they had Häyhänen flown to Washington where he could be interrogated by high-level officials of the FBI.

When asked why he defected, Major Häyhänen said he had grown tired of the espionage life and was ready to defect to America. He failed to mention that his superior had recently complained to Moscow about his shoddy performance, requesting he be recalled to Russia. In essence, Häyhänen feared for his life.

Häyhänen proved to be a gold mine of information about the Soviet spy ring in the US, even though he knew his two superiors only by their code names—"Mikhail" and "Mark." The FBI was visibly disappointed they had nothing further to go on. Häyhänen then recalled that he knew the location of "Mark's" art studio in Brooklyn. Suddenly, the FBI realized the master spy had committed a *faux pas* of immense proportions.

The standard, inviolable rule in the espionage world is never let anyone—not even a fellow spy—know where you are living. It was through this lapse that American authorities eventually learned of Colonel Rudolf Ivanovich Abel—a high-ranking KGB intelligence officer with a name straight from a Dostoevsky novel, as were his scarecrow-like features and stern demeanor, who was undoubtedly the most prolific Soviet spy to have ever pierced the shores of America.

Abel was a citizen of Russia and an influential colonel in the KGB. The KGB had assigned him the code name "Mark" for his communications with other Soviet agents. A decade earlier, he had entered the US illegally through a porous gap along the Canadian border. Abel, whose cover was that of a photographer and artist, lived in various hotels and apartments in New York City, and he maintained an art studio in Brooklyn, where he kept most of his tools of espionage—a shortwave radio and various devices concealing secret, and often encrypted, messages in small, hollowed-out containers. To disguise his identity, he adopted two creative aliases: "Emil Robert Goldfus"—an infant who had died in New York City in 1903—and "Martin Collins"—a fictitious individual purportedly born in New York City. It was seventy-two years before American journalists found Abel's real name carved on his tombstone in Moscow's Donskoy Cemetery— Vilyam Genrikhovich Fisher.

Reino Häyhänen, Abel's betrayer, was given the code name "Vic" to conduct his clandestine activities in the US. For three years—from July 1949 to October 1952—Häyhänen lived in Finland and began to establish his identity as the American-born "Eugene Nicoli Maki."

The *real* Maki was born in Enaville, Idaho, on May 30, 1919, which meant that he was about the same age as Häyhänen. Ten years later, the parents of Eugene Maki became enamored of glowing reports about the socialist utopia in the so-called "modern" Russia, and the family sold everything they had and moved to Estonia.

In Moscow, plans were being carefully made for the *new* Maki—this one thoroughly trained in foreign espionage—to enter the scene. During the period of switching identities, Häyhänen was deadly serious about the development of his alternate persona—so serious that even his new wife did not know about his earlier life.

Before Häyhänen left the Soviet Union, he received extensive training in the techniques of espionage, both traditional and modern. He was given thorough instruction in the finer aspects of photography, with particular emphasis on "microdots"—photographic reduction of a document which can later be enlarged to a readable size—and "soft film"—ordinary film chemically treated to remove its backing, rendering it pliable and capable of being folded to a very small size. Häyhänen was taught how to carefully secrete messages in tiny, hollowed-out objects such as coins, bolts, screws, and matchbooks for transmission to the USSR. He was also given training in cryptography for transmitting exceptionally sensitive information in a code difficult to break if accidentally apprehended.

On July 3, 1951, the thirty-one-year-old Häyhänen traveled to the American embassy in Helsinki, Finland, and presented a birth certificate showing that he was born as "Eugene Nicoli Maki" in Enaville, Idaho, on May 30, 1919. In the presence of a vice consul, Häyhänen executed an affidavit in which he explained that his family had left the United States for Estonia when he was ten years old, that he accompanied his mother until her death, and that he then left Estonia for Finland. A year later, the US embassy in Helsinki issued Häyhänen a passport, and several months after that, he sailed aboard the *Queen Mary*, arriving at New York City on October 21, 1952, ready to serve the Soviet Union as a KGB agent.

Several weeks before he departed for America, Häyhänen was sent to Moscow for further training. He was told that a Soviet agent—whose code name was "Mikhail"—would initially serve as his mentor in this country. In order to establish contact with "Mikhail," Häyhänen was instructed to go immediately after he arrived in New York to a restaurant known as Tavern on the Green in Central Park. Nearby, he would find a signpost marked "Horse Carts," and he was to place a small, red thumbtack there to indicate that he had arrived safely. If he suspected he was under surveillance, he was to use a white thumbtack instead.

For a year and a half—from the fall of 1952 until early 1954—"Mikhail" served as Häyhänen's superior in New York. They met only when necessary, at the subway station at Prospect Park. To exchange messages and intelligence data, they used "dead drops"—inconspicuous hiding places—in the New York City area. One of these drops was an iron picket fence at the end of 7th Avenue near Macombs Dam Bridge, and another was the base of a lamppost in Fort Tryon Park.

Häyhänen had been sent to the states to eventually serve as the chief assistant to an individual whom he then knew only as

"Mark"—who was, of course, the now-infamous Rudolf Ivanovich Abel. Häyhänen did not actually see Abel for another six months—until the summer of 1954—when the two met in the men's smoking room at a theatre in Flushing, New York. After that, Häyhänen saw Abel frequently, received his salary from him, and quietly carried out numerous discrete missions at his direction. Häyhänen carefully watched Abel use the predesignated drops for top-secret messages to other agents, and Abel informed Häyhänen that several agents were working for him. Abel told Häyhänen that he received coded messages from the Soviet Union, and on one occasion, Häyhänen observed Abel trying to receive signals on a shortwave radio.

The activities of Abel on behalf of the Soviet government were unquestionably extensive. For instance, sometime between July and December 1954, Abel received urgent instructions from Moscow to find Roy Rhodes—whose code name was "Quebec"—an American who had been turning over secret military information to the Soviets while he worked as a mechanic for the US embassy in Moscow. Rhodes's wife supposedly owned several businesses in Red Bank, New Jersey, but Abel and Häyhänen were unable to find Roy there. They later discovered that Rhodes's family had moved to Salida, Colorado, where Häyhänen traveled to search for Roy. Häyhänen learned from Rhodes's father and sister that Roy had moved to Tucson, but Häyhänen never had time to follow the lead.

In April 1957—after almost five years of espionage work in the US—Häyhänen boarded the ocean liner *Liberté* and sailed from New York to Europe on vacation. Shortly after arriving in Paris, he notified Soviet agents that he was proceeding to West Berlin. Instead, he went straight to the American embassy, where he informed the staff of his espionage activities on behalf of the Soviet government.

The apprehension and prosecution of one Rudolf Ivanovich Abel for high crimes of espionage against the United States was about to begin.

CHAPTER ONE

It was May 18, 1957, when Rudolph Abel registered at the Hotel Latham on East 28th Street near Fifth Avenue under the pseudonym of "Martin Collins."

A slightly built and peculiar little man with the hint of a British accent, Abel proceeded to rent Room 839 for twenty-eight dollars a week, payable at the end of each week on Saturday. The room was roughly ten feet wide and thirteen feet deep, and it contained a double bed, a low chest of drawers, a small desk, two chairs, and a folding baggage rack. A clothes closet, with a door, protruded into the bedroom. A small bathroom was attached.

A month later, on Friday, June 21, at 7:30 a.m., there was a sharp knock on the door followed by a quiet voice calling "Martin Collins," which awakened Abel. The night had been warm, and Abel had been sleeping naked on top of the sheets. Without putting on any clothes, he unbolted the latch and slowly cracked the door to see who was there. The three men outside pushed their way into the dark confines of the room to apprehend a suspect they had been closely trailing for a month. Once inside, they told Abel they were special agents from the Manhattan office of the FBI, and they quickly flashed their badges. Little did these agents realize at the time how prolific a Soviet spy Abel had been.

Abel assumed the men were armed, but he did not see any weapons. The agents ordered Abel to sit down on the bed, and he did, still naked. For the next five minutes, the three men—Paul Blasco, Edward Gamber, and Joseph Phelan—told Abel that they knew all about his activities and his accomplices. They urged Abel to "cooperate," or else he would be arrested. Abel replied that he did not know what they were talking about, and that he had a right under the US Constitution to remain silent. After a few minutes, Abel received permission to put on underwear.

As the FBI agents stood over the fifty-three-year-old Russian spy, Abel was no doubt searching his mind to determine how they found him. It must have occurred to him there was only one possibility—Reino Häyhänen, who had recently returned to Moscow, ostensibly on vacation, but also coincidentally after Abel had complained about the poor quality of his work. It must have also occurred to Abel that in a careless moment he had shown Häyhänen his art studio in Brooklyn, or none of this would be happening.

Throughout the questioning, the FBI agents derisively addressed Abel as "colonel," even though Abel had never used that title in the states. At no time did the FBI agents place Abel under arrest. After ten minutes, one of the FBI agents said to bring in the others. The agent opened the door and called in two officers from the Immigration and Naturalization Service—Edward Boyle and Edward Farley—and the FBI agents left.

The INS officers presented Abel with a warrant for his arrest as an alien illegally living in the United States. When asked his name, Abel replied, "Martin Collins." Two more INS agents—Lennox Kanzler and Robert Schoenenberger—then entered the room.

The officers handed Abel another document issued by the INS to commence deportation proceedings against Abel. The document informed Abel of a hearing at 70 Columbus Avenue in Manhattan on July 1, 1957, at 2:30 p.m. Both papers were addressed to Abel as "Martin Collins alias Emil Goldfus." At the agents' request, Abel acknowledged service of the papers by signing his name as "Martin Collins."

Abel's room was now crowded. The immigration officers handcuffed Abel and proceeded to search his room for any documents related to his alienage. Officer Boyle later described in an affidavit the contents of Abel's wallet:

> *That immediately following the service of the Warrant of Arrest, he [Officer Boyle] went to the clothes closet in "Collins" room and started to search his effects which were contained therein. That during this search, in a valise he observed a wallet and thereupon he searched the same. That among the items which he found in the wallet were several slips of paper, two being typewritten and one handwritten. That the handwritten note made reference to a symbol appearing on a pole opposite an address and set forth the time and place of a meeting. That one of the typewritten notes contained a question: relating to a picture and a response relating to a pipe and book. That the other typewritten note contained the names of two individuals having addresses in the USSR.*

The search of Abel's was conducted primarily by the INS, but the FBI agents remained in the room throughout the search. The INS found several birth certificates and a few other papers of interest, and they placed them in a file. They also searched the clothes he had worn the night before, which were piled on top of the bureau. They opened the clothes closet and removed Abel's suitcases, spreading their contents on the bed. All of Abel's belongings in the bureau were removed, searched, and packed into his suitcases. The toilet articles in the bathroom were also searched and packed. Abel would never see the objects again.

Abel was ordered by the men to collect his things, and while he was doing so, sharp-eyed FBI agents noticed that he was not only quietly trying to stuff cryptography pads and microfilm into the sleeves of his shirt, but that he had thrown a number of items away in the wastebasket. Abel would later brag that he was able to flush the most incriminating pieces of evidence down the toilet after he asked the agents for a bathroom break.

* * *

An affidavit of one of the FBI agents who later searched Abel's hotel room confirmed the presence of several incriminating documents and devices:

1. A Hallicrafters shortwave radio.
2. New York state birth certificate number 33318 in the name of "Emil Robert Goldfus," born August 2, 1902.
   [The agent noted that in the course of his investigation, he had seen a certificate and record of death reflecting that Emil Goldfus, a white male, died at the age of two months and seven days on October 9, 1902. It thus appeared that the true Emil Robert Goldfus died as an infant in 1902, and that his identity had been assumed by the individual using the name of Emil R. Goldfus, also known as Martin Collins, at the time of his arrest by immigration officers.]
3. New York City birth certificate purportedly issued in the name of Martin Collins.
4. An international certificate of vaccination issued in the name of Martin Collins on May 21, 1957.
5. A piece of graph paper containing eight rows of numbers, in groups of five digits.
   [The FBI agent noted that messages of this type, containing numerical code, are often used in connection with foreign intelligence activities.]
6. A scrap of paper containing the printed message:
   "I bought a ticket to next ship—Queen Elisab for next Thursday—1.31. Today I could not come because 3 men are tailing me."

7. A scrap of paper containing a handwritten note:

   "In Mex.: Signal 'T' on pole opposite # 191 Chihnaahva (Chihvahaa) St (Fonolia Roma), using side of pole towards roadway. Sat or Sun, Tues, Thur. Met on Mon, Wed, Fri at 3 PM movie 'Balmora.'"

   Another slip of paper containing the typewritten message:

   "'Balmora,' Avenida Oberon. 3 p.m. Display left of entrance. 'Is this an interesting picture?'. L. 'Yes. Do you wish to see it, Mr. Brandt?'. L smokes pipe and has red book in left hand."

   [The FBI agent noted that the first of these messages was likely an arrangement for a meeting place, and the second message appeared to contain a typical prearranged verbal exchange used to identify intelligence agents meeting for the first time.]

8. A slip of paper containing the typewritten message:

   "Mr. Vladinec, P. O. Box 348. M-w, K-9. USSR. Sign 'Arthur'. W. Merkulow, Poste Restante, M-a, USSR (Russia). Sign 'Jack.'"

9. A torn slip of paper containing the message:

   ". . . will w . . . in London 2–3 day while your message arrives. P"

10. Two wooden pencils and one mechanical pencil, which had been fashioned into "containers" of the type used by Soviet espionage agents secreting and transmitting messages, commonly on microfilm.

* * *

After an hour of questioning Abel, Officer Farley asked him which suit he would like to wear. Abel chose a particular gray suit, and Officers Farley and Boyle first searched the coats and pants. As Farley was packing Abel's possessions, he asked Abel if there was anything in the room he did not own, and Abel replied "no." Farley's affidavit described what happened next:

> *I therefore started packing everything into his suitcases. The alien became displeased as to the manner in which I had packed his belongings, and therefore requested permission to repack. This permission was granted, and he started to fold each item of clothing carefully and place them in his suitcases. He also placed his other belongings carefully in his suitcases. While he was packing, he at times would pick up objects which were lying about in the room and cast them into a wastebasket. By the time he finished packing, the wastebasket contained quite a few discarded items and was about half filled.*

The INS officers led Abel out of the room. Before leaving, Abel authorized the officers to pay his rent through that day, and he was checked out of the hotel. Abel and the four INS agents left the hotel by a rear door and entered a waiting sedan. Farley drove the car, Knazler and Schoenenberger sat in the front seat, and Abel and Boyle were in the back seat. The men arrived at immigration headquarters at 70 Columbus Avenue, where Abel was fingerprinted and photographed.

The FBI agents remained at the hotel and were granted permission by the hotel manager to return to the room, which they proceeded to ransack. In the process, they found a treasure trove of undercover spy paraphernalia beyond their most vivid imagination: encrypted messages, hollowed-out containers for secret messages, and microfilm. They gathered it up and cataloged it for use as evidence in Abel's inevitable trial.

Rudolf Abel under custody.

AP Images

Abel was held at INS headquarters until about 4:30 p.m., when he was taken by car to an airport near Newark, New Jersey. At the airport, Abel entered a Douglas DC-3, in which he and two immigration officers were the only passengers. Abel asked about their destination, and the men stated that they did not know. Abel's handcuffs were removed while he was aboard the plane. The plane stopped five hours later, and Abel believed that it was in Alabama. At approximately 4:30 a.m. the next morning, they arrived at what Abel learned was Brownsville, Texas. Here Abel was handcuffed, and the three men entered a waiting car which was accompanied by another car, and they drove sixty miles to McAllen, Texas. There Abel was placed in solitary confinement in a federal detention camp for aliens.

After two hours' sleep, Abel was given breakfast, and at about 9:00 a.m., he was led to a room where he was questioned until midafternoon by Officers Seely and Judge. The following day, Abel was questioned by Agents Blasco and Gamber (two of the FBI agents who had first entered his room in the Hotel Latham) and then by officers Seely and Judge. Abel refused to say anything.

The same procedure was repeated on Monday, June 24th. On Tuesday, June 25th, Abel decided to admit that his real name was Rudolf Ivanovich Abel and that he was a Russian citizen. He explained that he had found a large sum of American money in a ruined blockhouse in Russia, that he then bought a forged American passport in Denmark, and that he illegally entered the United States from Canada in 1948.

The agents ended the questioning and told Abel that he could see a lawyer. That afternoon, a lawyer in McAllen visited Abel in the detention camp. On June 27th, accompanied by counsel, Abel appeared before immigration officials at a hearing. Abel stated that he had entered the country illegally from Canada in 1948 and that during his residence in the states he had used the names "Emil Goldfus" and "Martin Collins." Abel was asked to state the country to which he wished to be deported, and he said "the USSR."

* * *

For almost three weeks, Abel was questioned daily by various FBI agents. They repeated the offer that if Abel would cooperate, he would receive fine food, expensive liquor, an air-conditioned room in a Texas hotel, and eventually a job with the US government. This was obviously an effort to turn Abel into a double agent serving the interests of the United States. Abel still refused to talk.

While in his cell at McAllen, Abel was given two typewritten lists of the property seized in his hotel room. During his sixth week in McAllen, he was served by Agent Joseph Phelan of the FBI with a criminal warrant for his arrest. Abel was informed of an indictment dated August 7, 1957, that charged him with the crime of espionage, and Abel understood that this was a capital offense. He was then brought before a US commissioner in Edinberg, Texas, and Abel waived extradition to New York. He was promptly flown to the federal house of detention in Manhattan and held in maximum security.

On August 9th, Abel appeared in US district court for the eastern district of New York, and the judge ordered that a plea of "not guilty" be entered on his behalf. Abel requested that the court assign him counsel. James Donovan was recommended by the local bar association, which asked him to defend Abel. The lawyers discussed with Abel the search and seizure of his property at the Hotel Latham, explaining what they considered to be the applicable law. Abel instructed them to institute whatever legal proceedings were appropriate and to assert any rights which he possessed under the Constitution and laws of the United States.

* * *

In an affidavit seeking a search warrant for Abel's possessions in his art studio in Brooklyn, a special agent of the FBI put the case against Abel this way:

"Emil R. Goldfus,' also known as 'Martin Collins,' has for a number of years since 1948 and continuously up until the date of his arrest on June 21, 1957, engaged in a conspiracy to violate Title 18, United States Code, Sections 793, 794, and 951.

"In furtherance of the conspiracy, 'Emil R. Goldfus' concealed in his studio at Room 505, on the fifth floor of the building located at 252 Fulton Street, Brooklyn, New York, a shortwave radio and related radio equipment; camera equipment, including microfilm and microdot equipment; bolts, earrings, batteries, cuff links, pencils, and similar items which have been or are suitable to be fashioned into 'containers' for the secreting and transmitting of microfilm, microdot, and other secret messages; and tools with which to fashion such 'containers;' and microfilm, microdot, and other messages, including coded communications; and other material intended for use, or which is or has been used, as a means of committing these crimes."

CHAPTER TWO

The arrest of Colonel Rudolf Abel was undoubtedly a big catch for the FBI. Having directed the entire Soviet espionage program in North America for nine years, Abel was clearly the highest-ranking Soviet agent to have ever been apprehended by the agency. At the height of the Cold War, Abel had been in charge of KGB activities in North America for nine years, and he had presumably transmitted to Russia a sizable amount of information detrimental to American security interests.

Allen Dulles, who was the head of the CIA during Abel's arrest, poignantly noted that,

> "There was little resemblance between the exploits of Ian Fleming's hero, the unique James Bond, in On Her Majesty's Secret Service, which I read with great pleasure, and the retiring and cautious behavior of the Soviet spy in the United States, Colonel Rudolf Abel. The intelligence officer, as distinct from the agent, does not usually carry weapons, concealed cameras, or coded messages sewed into the lining of his pants, or, for that matter, anything which would betray him if he should be waylaid. He should not permit himself to become the target of luscious dames who approach him in bars or come out of closets in hotel rooms. If this were to happen, he would probably be withdrawn from his particular mission because one of his main principles is to avoid being identified as an intelligence officer, except by those who work for him."

Colonel Abel was certainly no James Bond. He carried no handgun, Walther or otherwise, and he had no secret pockets sewn in his clothes. He lived a monochromatic existence that extended all the way to his gray pants, gray jacket, and gray fedora in an appearance that virtually defied any identity. He owned no fancy sports car and held no membership in an exclusive polo club. He was rail-thin, smoked a constant stream of cigarettes, and had an incurable sinus problem. His only hobbies were drawing and playing the guitar, and, by all accounts, he was not very accomplished at either one. He had a wife and daughter in Moscow, but he saw them so infrequently they would have practically forgotten him, except for the luxury they lived through his high-level employment in the Communist Party.

To fly below the radar of US authorities, Abel lived a quiet and austere existence. James Donovan, his court-appointed lawyer, noted that Abel was "just a face in the crowd, a name in a register, a silent figure in the majority legion who plod out our lives with uncomplaining, unobtrusive anonymity." Had it not been for Abel's brief—and exceptionally careless—disclosure of the location of his studio apartment to junior agent Reino Häyhänen, he might not have ever been discovered.

After Abel was arrested and arraigned, the judge asked the Brooklyn bar association to make a recommendation for court-appointed counsel. The name of James Donovan, a former commander in naval intelligence, a Harvard Law graduate, and a well-respected practitioner who had been a prosecutor in the Nuremburg trials, quickly surfaced. Despite strong protestations from Donovan's wife and friends, who urged him not to represent a Communist spy intent upon harming the United States, Donovan agreed to take the case.

The Department of Justice prepared an indictment, and in typical grandiose legal style, it leveled a series of terse accusations, alleging that Abel was part of an active conspiracy to commit espionage against US security interests. Most of the general allegations in the indictment spoke of how Abel and his associates—working under alias names, of course—met at certain obscure locations or left secret messages at designated "drops" to conduct their spy business. The indictment stated that:

- In 1948 and thereafter, Rudolf Ivanovich Abel—also known as "Mark," "Martin Collins," and "Emil R. Goldfus"—"unlawfully, willfully, and knowingly" conspired with Reino Häyhänen—also known as "Vic"—and other individuals to collect and deliver to the USSR "certain documents, writings, photographs, plans, maps, models, notes, instruments, appliances, and information" relating to the national defense of the United States of America, and particularly information regarding arms, equipment, and disposition of the US Armed Forces, as well as the US atomic energy program, with the intent to use that information to the advantage of the USSR.

- Abel and his co-conspirators "activated" as agents within the United States certain members of the US Armed Forces who were in a position to acquire information about the national defense of the United States, and would then "communicate, deliver, and transmit" such information to the USSR.

- To further the conspiracy, Abel and his co-conspirators used shortwave radios to send such information to the USSR.

- Abel and his co-conspirators fashioned "containers" from bolts, nails, coins, batteries, pencils, cufflinks, earrings, and the like by hollowing out concealed chambers in such devices to secrete microfilm, microdot, and other secret messages.

- Abel and his co-conspirators communicated with each other by enclosing messages in these containers and depositing them in prearranged "drop" points in Prospect Park in Brooklyn, Fort Tryon Park in New York City, and elsewhere.

- Abel and his co-conspirators received from the USSR sizable sums of money to conduct their illegal activities, and some of these funds were buried in the ground in New York and elsewhere.

- Abel and his co-conspirators assumed the identities of certain US citizens, both living and dead, and used birth certificates and passports in the names of those US citizens to communicate with each other through the use of numerical and other secret codes.

- Abel and certain of his co-conspirators set up clandestine radio posts for transmitting and receiving messages so that the USSR could be furnished with information relating to the national defense of the US.

* * *

The indictment listed in chronological order the acts that Abel and his co-conspirators committed to further the conspiracy:

- In 1948 Abel entered the United States at an unknown point along the Canadian border.

- In the summer of 1952, Häyhänen met with co-conspirators named Vitali Pavlovin and Mikhail Svirin at the headquarters of the Committee of Information in Moscow.

- On October 21, 1952, Häyhänen disembarked from the liner *Queen Mary* in New York City.

- In October of 1952, Häyhänen went to Central Park in Manhattan and left a secret message in the vicinity of the restaurant known as the Tavern on the Green.

- In 1952, Häyhänen went to Prospect Park in Brooklyn and left a secret message.

- In November of 1952, Häyhänen went to Fort Tryon Park in New York City and left a secret message.
- In December of 1952, Häyhänen met with Svirin at Prospect Park in Brooklyn.
- In the summer of 1953, Svirin handed Häyhänen a package of soft film.
- On December 17, 1953, Abel rented a small art studio on the fifth floor of the building located at 252 Fulton Street in Brooklyn.
- In August or September of 1954, Abel met with Häyhänen at RKO Keith's Theater in Flushing, Long Island.
- In or about the summer of 1954, Abel traveled by automobile to New Hyde Park, Long Island.
- In March or April of 1955, Abel and Häyhänen traveled by automobile from New York City to Atlantic City, New Jersey.
- In or about the spring of 1955, Häyhänen traveled by automobile from New York City to Quincy, Massachusetts, at the direction of Abel.
- In December of 1954 or January of 1955, Häyhänen traveled by rail from New York City to Salida, Colorado, at the direction of Abel.
- In the spring of 1955, Abel and co-conspirator Häyhänen traveled from New York City to the vicinity of Poughkeepsie, New York, for the purpose of locating a suitable site for a shortwave radio.
- In or about the spring of 1955, Abel gave a shortwave radio to co-conspirator Häyhänen in the vicinity of 252 Fulton Street in Brooklyn.
- In 1955 Abel brought a coded message to Häyhänen and requested him to decipher said message.

- In February of 1957, Abel gave Häyhänen a false birth certificate and $200 in the vicinity of Prospect Park in Brooklyn.

* * *

The Abel case encompassed almost every possible aspect of an espionage plot gone wrong. There was a lazy and inept young Soviet spy with a thick Finnish accent who had a serious drinking problem and who eventually decided to defect to the US, revealing everything he had done in the states for the last five years. There was a veteran, senior Russian spy who was extremely disciplined, but who made the fatal mistake of revealing his location to the rogue junior spy. There was an American serviceman stationed at the American embassy in Moscow who turned traitor and gave classified military information to the Russians in return for money and sex. And now the American authorities had captured the master spy, along with mounds of incriminating evidence.

Donovan later wrote in his book about the trial:

"Our objective was to show that in making the arrest the immigration officers were pawns of the FBI. Furthermore, we tried to establish that the raid and arrest, made without proper criminal warrants, were an FBI subterfuge to seize Abel and his belongings and keep the fact secret as long as possible. Had Abel 'cooperated' it would have been a brilliant counter-espionage coup. When the bold maneuver failed, however, and the Justice Department elected to prosecute, it forgot—and wanted to forget—that it had already violated the man's constitutional rights if he should be tried for a criminal offense under the law."

The prosecution's case revolved largely around the testimony of Reino Häyhänen, Abel's subordinate who had defected to the United States. Due to a surprising lapse by a spy as accomplished as Abel, Häyhänen had learned of the location of Abel's art studio in Brooklyn. It was also by Häyhänen's own incompetence that a local newsboy acquired a hollowed-out nickel containing an encrypted messaged to Häyhänen—physical evidence that figured prominently at Abel's trial.

It was Häyhänen's initial refusal to testify against his former superior officer in a grand jury investigation that led the FBI to enlist the assistance of the INS in Abel's arrest. Abel was surrounded by the tools of his trade, ample evidence to support espionage charges. The indictment eventually led to Abel's criminal trial for espionage, and it was conducted only three months after Abel's arrest.

The trial lasted ten days and had many dramatic moments. Abel, not unexpectedly, refused to take the witness stand. The government was forced to stake most of its case on the testimony of two individuals—Reino Häyhänen, the Soviet informant, and Roy Rhodes, the traitorous American soldier. The prosecution called twenty-seven witnesses (mostly FBI agents and INS officers), and over a hundred exhibits were introduced into evidence.

On October 25, 1957, the jury deliberated for only three-and-a-half hours before finding Abel guilty on all three counts of the indictment for conspiring to obtain and transmit national defense information to the Soviet Union as an unregistered foreign agent (the first count carried the death sentence). Abel was sentenced to thirty, fifteen, and five years in prison and given fines of $2,000 and $1,000. The sentences were to run concurrently, which meant a prison sentence of thirty years. For a fifty-five-year-old, this was equivalent to life imprisonment. For years afterwards, the case went up on appeal to the Second Circuit and the US Supreme Court, both of which affirmed Abel's conviction.

This is the story of Abel's tortuous journey through the American judicial system.

CHAPTER THREE

In November of 1948, a Cunard liner christened RMS *Scythia* quietly departed from the small port at Cuxhaven, Germany, bound for the shores of Quebec.

When the ship arrived in Canada a week later, it was a gray, blustery day, and the disembarking passengers braced themselves against the cold wnd as they quickly departed the ship. One of those passengers presented his passport to customs officials as "Andrew Kayotis"—which was not his real name—and he informed the authorities he was on his way to Detroit.

"Kayotis" was in his mid-forties and five feet, ten inches tall, with wiry, sharp features. He was otherwise unremarkable, down to his drab, wrinkled wardrobe consisting of gray pants, gray sport coat, and gray fedora. He easily blended in with the bustling crowd, which is exactly what he wanted.

"Kayotis" was to serve as an "illegal" intelligence officer for the USSR who, posing as a resident citizen of the US with an elaborately concocted and verifiable personal history, called a "legend," lived an undistinguished life to establish himself in a job with no connection to his real mission. Spy expert Jason Matthews has written that,

> "Preparing a legend (classically done by taking over the identity of a long-ago deceased person) is painstaking—living

it for years must be dementing. [...] Illegals are frightfully expensive to deploy and maintain. Their training must be rigorous. Communications and security are critical—there is no diplomatic immunity if an NKVD illegal is arrested. Less-than-fluent foreign language skills are a liability. Balanced against this inefficient, expensive, and risky method of deploying a spy is the significant advantage of a water-tight personal history, anonymity, and invisibility."

"Kayotis" was, in fact, one Vilyam Genrikhovich Fisher, a Soviet spy who later took the name of Rudolf Ivanovich Abel, among several other pseudonyms. The real Kayotis had conveniently died a year earlier in his native Lithuania.

Vilyam Genrikhovich Fisher was born in 1903 in what was then the outskirts of the village of Newcastle upon Tyne in northern England. He was known then as "Willie" Fisher, the son of Heinrich Fisher, a metal worker of German ancestry who was born in Russia, but who would later move to England to found the Newcastle branch of Russian Social Democratic Workers' Party and assist in the publication of the party organ. The Fishers were true Bolsheviks.

Willie's family moved from England back to Moscow when Willie was a teenager. As a youth, Abel showed strong aptitude for engineering and the arts. He had a flair for languages and became fluent in Russian, English, German, Polish, and Yiddish. Willie grew up, and at some point he took the name of Rudolf Ivanovich Abel—perhaps because it sounded more Russian—and he had his mind set on working for the KGB someday. He eventually married Elya and had a daughter, Evelyn.

Abel was a perfect fit for his eventual role as a spy in the West. His early upbringing in England provided him with a natural fluency in English that he was able to use to full avail. The fact that he had a wife and child in Moscow was further assurance to the KGB that he was not likely to defect. And he was a perfectionist, totally dedicated, loyal to the Soviet cause.

Abel somehow managed to survive the Stalinist purge, and with a distinguished record in World War II, he became an "illegal" KGB intelligence officer—one who was formally unassociated with the Soviet agency. He was active in Oslo and London before he moved to America, where he ran all Soviet espionage activities in North America for nine years.

Russian spies, it seems, are true ideologues. In his book *The Craft of Intelligence*, Allen Dulles, the former director of the CIA, noted about Russian spies,

"From my own experience I have the impression that the Soviet intelligence officer represents the species Homo Sovieticus in its unalloyed and most successful form. This strikes me as much the most important thing about him, more important than his characteristics as a practitioner of the intelligence craft itself. It is as if the Soviet intelligence officer were a kind of final and extreme product of the Soviet system, an example of the Soviet mentality pitches to the nth degree."

This certainly seemed to be the case with Rudolf Abel, and it animated everything he did. He trained Red Army radio operators during World War II, and he was quickly drafted by Soviet intelligence. After Abel was rewarded for his wartime performance as an illegals officer, he was groomed for the most prestigious posting of the NKVD (*Narodnyi Komissariat Vnutrennikh Del*, the People's Commissariat for Internal Affairs), the leading Soviet secret police organization and precursor to the KGB: a position in the United States of America.

When Abel arrived in the states in 1948, his goal was to revitalize the network of atomic spies which, since 1942, had been providing classified information from the Manhattan Project research labs at Los Alamos, New Mexico, but whose productivity had been thwarted by postwar security enhancements. For his first two years, Abel established himself, received instructions from Moscow, and undoubtedly traveled to Santa Fe to reactivate old sources of information and establish new informants who could deliver information to an illegal, who would then transmit reports to Moscow. This arrangement would ensure that there was no apparent Soviet involvement, preserving anonymity and communication to and from NKVD headquarters.

Abel lived in a variety of boarding houses and hotels in New York City under several aliases—primarily "Emil R. Goldfus" and then "Martin Collins." He was forty-four years old, and he told those he met, which were few in number, that he was a retired photographer who also liked to draw and paint. Abel first leased the premises at 216 West 99th Street in New York using the name of "Emil R. Goldfus," a baby who was born in Manhattan on August 2, 1902, and who died a little over a year later on October 9, 1903. Abel then moved to a four-story, red-brick building on the West Side while he looked for useful information, such as transportation systems, and searched for secluded drop sites where he could leave microfilmed messages in hollowed-out containers.

Abel then moved to an apartment on Riverside Drive and 74th Street, and he signed the lease as "Goldfus" once again. For a very brief time, he took on another persona, where he was an Englishman who simply called himself "Milton." Perhaps he enjoyed the fact that he could convince people he was someone else and decided to take the challenge of assuming another identity.

Late in 1953, Abel left the Upper West Side and rented an apartment in Brooklyn. At this point, he had been in the US for five years. With the pseudonym still that of "Emil Goldfus," Abel rented an art studio in a seven-story building called Ovington Studios, on the edge of Brooklyn Heights. Like most of the other artists and writers who rented workspaces there, Abel lived elsewhere and came and went to draw and paint as he wished. His studio, number 509, was ten feet by fourteen feet, with pale green walls and wooden floor and lit by a bare light bulb. For his amusement, he kept his record player, guitar, and various books there. In a nearby storeroom, he kept a large work table, Hallicrafters shortwave radio, and the tools of his spy trade—camera lenses, nails, pliers, wrenches, cutting tools, acid, optical equipment, magnifying lens, and other miscellaneous items.

Abel never admitted to his attorney James Donovan that any of his activities in the US had been directed by party officials in Soviet Russia. He insisted that any of the information that he collected was of a general nature, and none involved military secrets. Abel called Häyhänen a "rat" for defecting and thereby embarrassing his family back home, and he said he could never imagine himself abandoning his country in order to save his own life.

CHAPTER FOUR

The KGB needed an assistant for Colonel Abel in the United States, and for this position it eventually chose Reino Häyhänen, whose background could have been created by a Hollywood scriptwriter. Born in 1920 into peasant circumstances on a farm near Petrograd, Häyhänen's family moved to Pushkin, about twenty-five miles from Leningrad, when Reino was thirteen years old.

The young Häyhänen was naturally bright, and he excelled in school. He became a member of the youth organization *Komsomol*, the junior Communist party, and he graduated from the Pedagogical Institute with honors in 1939. Dark-haired, handsome, and fit, he taught at an elementary school in Lipitzi for two months before he was drafted by the NKVD.

Häyhänen was fluent in Finnish, and he was assigned to the combat zone in order to translate intercepted documents and to interrogate prisoners during the Winter War, the brief military conflict between the Soviet Union and Finland. With the end of the war in 1940, he was given the responsibility of determining the loyalty of Soviet workers in Finland and to plant informants among them to identify anti-Soviet elements among the intelligentsia. His NKVD superiors were impressed with his work.

As a result, Häyhänen was accepted into membership in the Soviet Communist Party in May of 1943. At the end of World War

25

II in 1945, he rose to the rank of senior operational agent in the NKGB (*Narodny Komissariat Gosudarstvennoi Bezopasnosti*, the People's Commissariat for State Security), where his job was to identify dissident elements among the local citizens. Once again, he excelled in the field. For seven years, he had attended courses and meetings in counter-intelligence, and he had gone as far as he could in that field.

Reino Häyhänen

In the summer of 1948, Häy-hänen's break as an intelligence officer occurred when he was recruited to Moscow to do intelligence work for the prestigious KGB (*Komitet Gosudarstvennoy Bezopasnosti*, the Committee for State Security), the main security agency for the Soviet Union. Employment by the KGB was, in reality, military service, and its employees were governed by laws and regulations similar to that of the Soviet Army. The main functions of the KGB were foreign intelligence, counterintelligence, operative-investigative activities, guarding the borders of the USSR, and protecting the leadership of the Central Committee of the Communist Party and the Soviet government. The agency was also charged with quelling nationalism, dissent, and anti-Soviet activities.

Unlike the employment process for America's CIA, a Soviet citizen did not typically apply for a position in the intelligence service of the KGB. Instead, he was selected. Bright young men in various fields, whether it was foreign affairs, economics, or the sciences, were identified by Communist party superiors and proposed for work in intelligence. These prospective intelligence officers were either party members, candidates for party membership, or members of *Komsomol*. In addition to being bright, they had to maintain impeccable political credentials, with no trace of *"bourgeois taint"* or record of dissent in their family.

While he was in Moscow, Häyhänen met and married Aki-lina Pavlova, and he had a child with her. But shortly thereafter, the KGB had a new assignment for him, and it required him to completely sever his relationship with his family and study the English language. He would also receive intensive training in photographing documents and in encoding and decoding secret messages. In spite of the severe emotional costs to his family, Häy-hänen accepted without hesitation the new position, such was his devotion to the Communist Party.

While he was being trained in the KGB, Häyhänen worked as a mechanic in the city of Valga, Estonia. Finally, in the summer of 1949, he entered Finland through the Soviet naval base in Porkkala, outside of Helsinki. For three years, Häyhänen lived in Finland. He first worked in the northern province of Lapland as a blacksmith, and then in the southern cities of Tampere and Turku doing auto body work. Here Häyhänen began to carefully craft his new identity as the American-born "Eugene Maki" before he was transferred to the United States.

* * *

The original Eugene Nicolai Maki had been born in Enaville, Idaho, on May 30, 1919. Eugene's mother was born in America, but his father had immigrated from Finland to the United States in 1905. In the mid-1920s, the Makis heard glowing reports of conditions in contemporary Russia. They sold all their belongings and, along with young Eugene, left the Idaho farm to book passage on a passenger ship to Estonia.

As the years passed, even the older residents of Enaville, Idaho forgot about the Maki family. In Moscow, plans were made for a new "Eugene Maki"—one thoroughly versed in Soviet intelligence techniques—to prepare for a challenging espionage assignment in the United States. During this period, Häyhänen was careful to avoid attracting attention to himself. While in Finland, Häyhänen married Hannah Kurikka, a beautiful twenty-seven-year-old blonde from Siilinjärvi who knew her husband only as "Eugene Maki," so carefully did he conceal the details of his previous life.

Before he left the Soviet Union, Häyhänen received extensive training in the tactics of espionage. He was given instruction in the advanced science of photography, with particular emphasis on "microdots" and "soft film." The significance of microdots and soft film for espionage purposes was its ability for messages to be secreted in tiny, hollowed-out objects like coins, bolts, screws, and matchbooks. And he was given rigorous training in cryptography for coding sensitive information.

Häyhänen—now "Eugene Maki"—traveled to the American embassy in Helsinki, and there, in the presence of a vice consul, he executed an affidavit in which he explained that when he was ten years old, his family left the United States for Estonia, that he lived in Estonia with his mother until her death, and that he then left Estonia to live in Finland.

Based upon his affidavit, the US embassy in Helsinki issued Häyhänen a US passport under the name of "Eugene Maki," thinking that he was nostalgic for his childhood and wanted to return to the States, having been gone for some twenty-five years. A year later, the newly recreated "Eugene Maki" sailed aboard the *Queen Mary* for New York City, where he arrived on October 21, 1952, eager to serve his homeland in the important job of stealing sensitive military data from the USA.

* * *

The compelling story of Reino Häyhänen's background and his eventual assignment to the United States as a Soviet spy was revealed in some detail in the trial of Rudolf Abel. The prosecutor approached the witness and said, "Now, Mr. Häyhänen, I want to ask you to answer some specific questions more in detail. Where were you born?"

"I was born in Russia, it is about twenty-five miles from Leningrad, in a village, Kaskisarri," replied Häyhänen, in his broken English and heavy Baltic accent.

"What was the date of your birth?"

"Fourteenth of May, 1920."

"Were you educated in Russia?"

"Yes, I was."

"Will you tell us about your education?"

"I finished in Russia teacher's college."

"Did you thereafter teach school?"

"Yes, I was teaching just about three months, and then I was drafted to NKVD in 1939."

"At that time was the NKVD a part of the army?" asked the prosecutor.

"No, it was like secret police, NKVD. It was at that time militia and NKGB—they were together—and after that NKVD was divided to NKVD and NKGB."

"When you were drafted in November 1939, what branch of the NKVD were you assigned to?"

Häyhänen replied, "I was assigned as interpreter to operations group on Finnish territory, what was occupied by the Russian troops after Finnish-Russian War in 1939."

"Do you speak Finnish?"

"Yes, I do."

"What were your duties in connection with this first assignment?"

"My duties were that I had to work as interpreter when NKVD officials been questioning some war prisoners," said Häyhänen.

"When you were first drafted in the NKVD, did you receive any training?"

"We got several lectures during that nine- or ten-day period. How to question war prisoners, how to try to find that maybe there is somebody who is a spy to send as a war prisoner. Then also we got short training as for future NKVD officials or workers—how to work on counterespionage work, how to find anti-Soviet people or some espionage agents from some other countries on Russian territory."

"After your first assignment as an interpreter in the NKVD, what did you next do?" the prosecutor asked.

"Then, after Finnish-Russian war ended, I was sent to Karelia for NKVD work. I was working as interpreter, and I was working as NKVD official, too."

"After that assignment was completed, what did you do?"

Häyhänen replied, "That assignment was completed 1948, and I was called to Moscow."

"Do I understand that from roughly 1939 to 1948 you were working for the NKVD or successor organizations, which changed names from NKGB to KGB?"

"That is right," agreed Häyhänen.

"During that period between 1939 and 1948 did you join the Communist Party of Russia?"

"Yes, I did."

* * *

The prosecutor continued the discussion of how Häyhänen's career suddenly veered toward one of true espionage, including stints in Estonia and Finland along the way.

"In the summer of 1948, were you summoned to Moscow?"

"Yes, I was called to Moscow. My bosses explained to me that now they need me, instead of counterespionage world, on espionage work."

"Were you advised of a change in assignment?" asked the prosecutor.

"Yes, they told that they need me now on espionage work because they can use me more on espionage work so that I can use my knowledge of Finnish."

"After your visit in Moscow, where did you go? Did you return home?"

"I returned to Karelia, and I prepared everything for moving from Karelia to Estonia."

"What work did you do in Estonia?"

"I received training on photography, then on driving car and how to make some repairs in cars—to show I can work as a car mechanic."

"Can you tell us, specifically, your training in photography?"

Häyhänen responded, "In photography, I got training as all photographers were getting. I was getting training on how to copy some photos, and then I got some training of using Minox cameras."

"Did you receive any other training in anything else while you were in Estonia?"

"I got training in to talk English, to write English."

"While you were in Estonia, did you find the location of your future assignment in espionage work?" asked the prosecutor.

"The location was the United States of America."

"At that time that you were in Estonia, did you receive information concerning a legend for yourself? Will you first explain what a legend is?"

"A legend is that for somebody who has to live another life by another name—that has to show himself for another person as he is," said Häyhänen.

* * *

The prosecutor asked Häyhänen, "In connection with the legend that you learned of in Estonia, what was done concerning that?"

"I was called second time to Moscow and there picked up legend for 'Eugene Nicoli Maki,' who really was born in this country and which his parents went to Russia in 1927. Legend for me was that from the day when I would go to Finland, I would have to live the life by the name 'Eugene Nicoli Maki.' I did it since 1949."

"Did I understand you to say that you went from Moscow to Finland?"

"Yes," replied Häyhänen.

"How did you travel to Finland? Will you describe that trip?"

"From Moscow I went to Estonia, and from Estonia I went by boat to Porkkala—was Finnish territory, but occupied by Russians," said Häyhänen.

"And from Porkkala where did you go?"

"From Porkkala then Russian espionage officials took me to Finnish Territory to Helsinki."

"How did you make that trip?"

"We made that trip in the car, and while they have been crossing that border I was in car trunk."

"In car trunk?" asked the prosecutor.

"Yes, in trunk of the car."

The prosecutor inquired further, "Now, what did you do in Finland?"

"In Finland, I was building my background for that legend. It means that I had to show that really I was in Finland since 1943 instead of 1949. I had to find some people who can tell if necessary that they meet me or I lived with them since 1943."

"Would you tell us how you went about establishing the legend?"

"To establish that legend, I lived about three months in Lapland, in northern part of Finland, and over there I found two people who have been willing to testify if necessary that I lived over there during the war," said Häyhänen.

"What years would that be?"

"Since 1943 up to 1948, because in 1948 then I moved to one blacksmith."

"Blacksmith?"

"Yes, repairman, and I lived over there, I worked over there for a while just to show some kind of connection that I really was working in Lapland. And then I moved to southern part of Finland. It was 1950."

"You mentioned seeing some people who would say that you had lived there?" asked the prosecutor.

"Yes."

"Did you pay them any money?"

"Yes, I did," replied Häyhänen.

"Was that your own money?"

"No, I got that money from Moscow."

"After you worked in 1949 and 1950 as a blacksmith, what did you do?"

"Then I moved to Tampere—that is Finnish town. I was working on safe factory. They have been building safes and automobile body work they have been doing, repair works," said Häyhänen.

"Was this all done as a part of your legend?"

"Yes, it was just to show that I am earning money by working on some other place, but not on espionage work."

The prosecutor continued. "After you had finished that work, what did you do?"

"Then from Tampere I moved to Turku. And when I lived in Turku after 1952, I applied for American passport, when my Moscow bosses—they have been certain that my background is well built—that it is now to apply for United States passport."

"Will you tell us how you applied for the passport?" asked the prosecutor.

"I applied first from Idaho, United States of America, a copy of birth certificate. Then I went to American Legation in Helsinki."

"What birth certificate did you write for in Idaho?"

"For 'Eugene Nicoli Maki.'"

"Then, as I understand you, you say you went to the American Embassy?

"That's right."

"Will you tell us what you did?"

Häyhänen replied, "Then over there, they asked me how long I was in Finland. And then they asked me to get some more papers that I never was serving in the army, especially Finnish army, that I never vote in Finland. So I got those papers, and by those papers I got American passport for coming to the United States."

Soon thereafter, Reino Häyhänen—aka "Eugene Nicoli Maki"—would sail for the shores of America to serve as a Soviet agent.

* * *

Reino Häyhänen arrived in the United States on October 21, 1952, and was assigned to an individual he only knew as "Mikhail." The assignment lasted for a year and a half. "Mikhail" taught Häyhänen how to use the various hidden locations (or "drops") in New York City.

In Abel's trial, the prosecutor asked Häyhänen, "How were you to report your arrival in the United States?"

"I reported it through 'drop,' and I explained that I arrived all right, but first report was that I had to put thumb tack in Central Park."

"Whereabouts in Central Park?" asked the prosecutor.

"It's close to Tavern on the Green where is that horse path, and there was the warning that 'Be careful, horse riding,' or something like that. I cannot remember exactly words."

"Will you explain what a 'drop' is?" requested the prosecutor.

"By a 'drop' I mean a secret place which you or several people know where you can hide some container. If I will hide container in that drop, and another person will pick up that container and will get it."

"Were you given the location of any drops in your instructions from Moscow?"

"Yes, I know several locations," replied Häyhänen.

"Will you tell us the locations of those drops which were given to you in your instructions?"

"Number one was located on Jerome Avenue, and then drop number two was located on Central Park."

"Where is the actual drop number one located? Is it behind the wall?"

Häyhänen responded, "It is between the cement wall, and behind that location there is hole."

"Did you use this drop during the entire time you were in the United States?"

"I was using it just once, I think, and same thing, that once I got message from Soviet officials. Because that drop was not convenient, I got them more convenient drops later."

"Where was drop number two located?"

"It was in Central Park under the bridge."

"What was that drop used for?"

"Communications with Soviet officials."

The judge interrupted, "What bridge are you talking about? I think there is more than one bridge in Central Park."

"This bridge is close to that water reservoir. If you enter that Central Park, it is around 110th Street, I think. I cannot tell you exactly," said Häyhänen.

"Was there another drop assigned?"

"Drop number three was located in Fort Tryon Park."

"Did you ever use this drop?"

"Yes, I was many times there."

* * *

The prosecutor asked Häyhänen, "What type of messages did you put in these drops?"

"I used the drops to report to my bosses what I did in a certain period, in a certain time, and how I did it—just to report what my bosses asked me to do."

"What containers did you use in the drops?"

Häyhänen explained, "Hollow bolts, coins, screws, flashlight batteries—that is many of what I was using—and matchbooks."

"Can you describe for the court and jury a coin container?"

"Yes," said Häyhänen, "a coin container is a hollow coin made from two coins, but made that way. If you look first at it that is a usual coin, but with needle you can open it, and there is space to hide some message on soft film or slip of paper."

"You used the term 'soft film.' Could you explain what soft film is?" asked the prosecutor.

"Soft film means that when you take some picture on original film that then you prepare soft film to put in dioxane, and when that film stays in there for several hours, it will become soft film. Just what you took picture will be on that film, but that cellophane will disappear from that film."

"In other words, originally it is on hard film, and that would be stiff?"

"Yes."

"And when you put it in that chemical you described, does it take the hardness out of it?"

"Yes, it does."

"And then, as I understand you to say, you can then fold it and put it in a container?"

"That is right."

The prosecutor sought clarification. "Were these messages in English or Russian or code?"

"Messages, I was getting in English and in Russian. I was getting both kind of messages."

"Now, messages that you sent—were they the same?"

"Yes, that is right. I was giving messages in English and in Russian."

"Now, did you send or receive any messages in code?"

Häyhänen replied, "In code, yes, I did. I was sending them and I was getting in code, several messages."

CHAPTER FIVE

After the muscular, square-jawed Reino Häyhänen had arrived in New York and worked for "Mikhail" for a year and a half, he was transferred to "Mark"—who Häyhänen would later learn was the notorious Rudolf Abel. Häyhänen would complete assignments for Abel for six months before even setting eyes on him.

Three drops had been assigned to Häyhänen by his superiors in Moscow; here he was to leave messages and look for assignments. One of these drops was in Central Park, another in the base of a lamppost in Fort Tryon, and the third was a hole between a sidewalk and a wall along Jerome Avenue, between 165th and 167th Streets, in the Bronx.

In addition, there were the "signal" areas to alert Häyhänen and others of the presence of messages: a streetlight in Brooklyn and a railway station in Newark. If Häyhänen left a horizontal chalk mark, it meant that he had a message for one of his superiors. A vertical chalk mark indicated that a message was waiting for Häyhänen at one of the drops.

* * *

In Abel's trial, the prosecutor asked Häyhänen about how he met Abel and how they worked together as spies. "Mr. Häyhänen, when did you first meet the defendant, 'Mark'?"

"First, I met him in men's smoking room in RKO Keith's Theater in Flushing," Häyhänen said.

"Will you fix a date, if you can, approximately?"

"It was July or August, 1954."

"Will you tell us about that first meeting? How was it brought about?" asked the prosecutor.

Häyhänen replied, "I got instructions, short message from Soviet officials through drop, and there was that somebody wants to meet me. So, like I testified yesterday, that meeting place was transferred to that RKO Keith's Theatre. So I went to that theatre that date—in the evening when it was in message, the date and time between 8:00 or 9:00 in the evening. I went to that men's smoking room wearing that blue tie with red stripes and was smoking a pipe. Then, 'Mark' came, and he then told 'let's go out,' and we been talking outside of the theatre. We been walking in Flushing. Then we went to one—"

The prosecutor interrupted. "Just a minute. If I may ask you this, did you say you were 'wearing the blue tie with the red stripes'?"

"That is right," said Häyhänen.

"Did you recognize 'Mark'?" asked the prosecutor.

"No, I didn't know 'Mark,' but he recognized me by that blue tie and that I was smoking a pipe, and there was nobody in that men's smoking room, nobody else."

The prosecutor continued. "Did you have a conversation when you first met him, immediately?"

"'Mark' should ask me passwords, but he didn't ask because he told that I know for sure whom he has to meet."

"What did he first say to you?" asked the prosecutor.

"'Hello', then he told me that 'never mind about passwords,' that 'I know that you are right man.'"

"In other words, as I understood you to say, he said, 'Let's go outside'?"

"Yes," confirmed Häyhänen.

"Did you go outside?"

"Yes, we been walking and then we went about three or four blocks from that movie theatre to restaurant where we been drinking coffee."

"Would you tell us about that conversation?"

"During that conversation, 'Mark' told that he got message that I arrived to New York City long ago. But he was surprised that so long it took that he got orders to meet me or to have this conversation. Then he explained that he was in this country already several years. What else it was? Let me see. Then, he asked if I had 'cover work.' I explained that I didn't have yet, and he told that we have to think about it because otherwise it will be difficult with time. Because if I work somewhere eight hours a day, I won't have enough time for espionage work."

"Would you explain what you mean by 'cover work' to the court and jury?"

Häyhänen elaborated, "By 'cover work,' I mean that kind of work that to show that I am earning money from that work, and like later, then, we decided about opening photo studio."

* * *

The prosecutor then asked Häyhänen, "At this first meeting, did 'Mark' tell you where he lived?"

"No," said Häyhänen.

"Did he tell you where he—whether he—worked or not?"

"Not in the first meeting. Then, later, in later meetings he told that he has income from small shop somewhere in Brooklyn."

The judge interjected, "Did he say what kind of a shop?"

Häyhänen replied, "He told that small shop, but he didn't explain it more carefully in more detail. Then, later, he told that he has storage place in Brooklyn—storage room for his equipment all that he has, and other things."

Donovan, Abel's lawyer, interrupted the questioning: "He has never identified the time or place of those meetings."

39

The judge curtly replied, "You know what cross-examination is, don't you? You are an experienced lawyer."

Donovan respectfully responded, "Your Honor, I also know when objections should be made to incompetent testimony."

The judge then ruled, "All right. Your objection is noted, and it is overruled."

The prosecutor resumed his questioning. "Do you remember when 'Mark' told you of the location of this storage room?"

Häyhänen replied, "'Mark' told about location of his storage room in 1955 when I moved to Newark, New Jersey. I found there one store with apartment, and we decided to open photo studio for me, like cover work, like photo studio."

"Did you ever visit the storage room?"

"Yes, I did, once."

"Will you tell us approximately when?" asked the prosecutor.

"It was in May 1955. And one evening, 'Mark' told that he has some photo equipment to give me, and let's go and take them from storage room. So, we came to Fulton Street, 252, on fourth or fifth floor, it was located that his storage room."

"You have testified now to the visit to the storage room. Did you ever on other occasions go to 252 Fulton Street?"

"Yes, then two times I came to the same place, but Mark already brought downstairs some more photo equipment, and I took them to the car—that photo equipment with Mark—and I took it to Newark, New Jersey," said Häyhänen.

"In addition to the photograph supplies that you said you picked up, did you pick up anything else at 252 Fulton Street from 'Mark'?"

"Yes, I picked up also shortwave radio."

"Did 'Mark' at any time tell you where he lived?"

"No, he never told where he lived exactly, but he mentioned that he lived, on several occasions, in hotels."

* * *

The prosecutor resumed his questions about Häyhänen's assignments for Abel.

"Did you receive a salary for your work in the United States?" asked the prosecutor.

"Yes, I did."

"Up to 1954, when you first met 'Mark,' how was your salary paid?"

"I was getting salary through drops."

The prosecutor asked, "After you met 'Mark,' how was your salary paid?"

"After I met 'Mark,' then 'Mark' was giving me my salary."

The prosecutor resumed the questioning. "You testified that 'Mark' gave you a shortwave radio. At the time that he gave it to you, did you have a conversation with him?"

Häyhänen replied, "Conversation was that he has to locate some place from where he can get shortwave radio messages. And then we took a trip to Croton Reservoir on Highway 129—about a hundred yards from the bridge, reservoir bridge."

"And when you arrived at the Croton Reservoir, what did you do?"

Häyhänen responded, "'Mark' put antenna to that radio, and he tried to get some—just to listen that it is possible to listen by that radio—some other stations, shortwave stations. But I don't know, maybe fuse was burned or something happened that he couldn't listen. And after that he told me that I may as well have that radio in my apartment because he has another radio."

"How did 'Mark' try to receive? Did he plug it in or—"

"We got converter from six volts to 110 volts, and we plug in the converter to cigarette lighter in the car."

"Could you tell us about the approximate time that this took place?" asked the prosecutor.

"That happened in the end of May, 1955, or in first days of June, 1955, before 'Mark' went to Moscow."

The prosecutor asked, "Mr. Häyhänen, in your testimony, you have used the phrase 'before 'Mark' went to Moscow.' Do you know whether 'Mark' did go to Moscow? Did you ever have a conversation with him about it, let's put it that way?"

"Yes," replied Häyhänen, "we had several conversations about his trip to Moscow. He went for Moscow, from my best recollection, 10th of June, 1955."

"Did 'Mark' tell you *how* he was going to Moscow?" asked the prosecutor.

"Yes, he did," said Häyhänen. "He told me that he has to go through Austria. And then when he came back from Moscow and we met again, he explained to me first he took a plane to Paris. From Paris by train he went to Austria, and from Austria, then I cannot remember exactly how he went from Austria."

* * *

Secure radio communications between an intelligence headquarters and agents in the field were assisted by the use of what were called "cipher pads." These cipher pads were individual sheets of printed rows and columns of five-digit numerical groups. The pads were greatly reduced in size for concealment purposes. A field agent would receive a shortwave radio broadcast from intelligence headquarters, and these were typically a monotone female voice reading a series of numbers, which was the encrypted message.

The agent would then subtract the recited numbers on an individual cipher pad whose only other key was in Moscow. The resulting numbers would correspond to the twenty-six letters of the alphabet and reveal the message. Each random page of the cipher pad was different and used only once, making it impossible for outsiders to discern patterns.

* * *

The prosecutor continued. "Now, getting back to the time that you first met him, Mr. Häyhänen, did you have subsequent meetings with 'Mark'?"

"Yes, I was meeting him once or twice a week."

"Do you know whether 'Mark' had any drops?"

"Yes, I know that he had several drops," replied Häyhänen.

"Will you tell us the location of those drops?" asked the prosecutor.

"His drop number four and drop number seven, they been located at 95th Street in front to Henry Hudson Parkway and Riverside Park."

"Did you ever visit those drops with 'Mark'?"

"Yes, we did several times," said Häyhänen.

"In addition to drops four and seven which you testified to, do you know whether 'Mark' had any other drops?"

"Yes, I know he had drop number six on Riverside Drive around 104th Street, I believe."

"What type of drop was that?" asked the prosecutor.

"It was for thumbtacks on the bench."

"Would you describe it just a little more, please?"

"There are benches for public, and underneath if you sit down to that bench to right side—so on the bench, in the middle bolt of bench—under that 'Mark' put thumbtack. Once he put message over there, and he showed how he is using it."

"Did you and he visit the drop together?" the prosecutor asked.

"Yes," said Häyhänen, "he had a message to send to Soviet officials, and he told that we have to drive over there, that he put thumbtack."

"Do you know the location of any other drop that the defendant had?"

"Then he had one drop in Central Park West, what we called 'walking drop.' It means that he could put under mailbox magnetic container from 74th Street up to 79th Street, as I remember."

"Did he say anything to you about who the messages were for?"

"He has to send messages to Soviet officials in those drops," said Häyhänen.

"Do you know any signal areas that Mark used?" inquired the prosecutor.

"One signal area he was using that fence on Central Park West and 81st Street. There is a fence around that museum."

The prosecutor asked, "Did 'Mark' use any meeting areas, to your knowledge?"

"Yes, he told that several times he met Soviet officials in Symphony Theatre, and in the same place they had drop number two—under carpet in movie theatre, in balcony."

"In other words, the Symphony Theatre was both a meeting place and a drop area?" said the prosecutor.

"Yes, and he explained that it is very convenient because it has two exits—one, that main entrance, is from Broadway, then to side street is exit."

"Did you ever visit this Symphony Theatre with the defendant?"

"Yes, once I was over there with him," said Häyhänen.

"Approximately when?"

"It was the springtime, 1955."

"The drop and the meeting area were inside the theatre, as I understand it?"

"That's right."

"Have you given us the location of all of Mark's drops that you know?"

"Numbers two, four, six, and seven. Yes, that's what I remember what he had," replied Häyhänen.

"Have you given us all the locations of Mark's meeting places that you know?"

44

"I knew only about this meeting place. At Symphony Movie Theatre."

The prosecutor wanted to make sure. "Have you given us the location of *all* of 'Mark's' signal areas that you know?"

"He explained that he had one signal place at dentist at some dentist's office, and he told that it was not convenient for him. Then, what I mentioned already, that signal area close to that 81st Street and Central Park West. Then one more signal area that—the latest one was 95th Street subway station, and it was—"

"Was it inside or outside the subway station?" asked the prosecutor.

"Inside, but I try to recall which line it was. It was Eighth Avenue Subway, in Manhattan."

"Did Mark give you—for your use—the location of a drop or bank at any time?"

"No," said Häyhänen.

* * *

Morton Sobell was an American engineer with General Electric who worked on military and government contracts, and in 1951 he was convicted and sentenced to thirty years in prison for spying on behalf of the Soviets as a part of a ring that included Julius Rosenberg, who stole secrets from the atomic bomb lab at Los Alamos. Morton's wife Helen was not prosecuted, but she remained sympathetic to the Russian cause. To recruit Helen Sobell as a Soviet spy, Abel was anxious to pay her $5,000 in cash that had been buried in a state park nearby.

The prosecution questioned Häyhänen about the unusual transaction.

"Now, prior to June, 1955, when you testified that 'Mark' went to Moscow, did you accompany him to any other location in the general vicinity of New York State?"

Häyhänen replied, "We been traveling in several states several occasions, just to we been taking some few photos. We been in New York State, New Jersey, Pennsylvania."

"Well, on one of these trips did you have occasion to go to Bear Mountain Park?"

"Yes, we did."

"Were you accompanied by the defendant?" asked the prosecutor.

"Yes."

"How did you go?"

"We went by the car."

The judge asked, "Did you have any conversation about or with 'Mark' concerning the trip to Bear Mountain?"

"Yes," said Häyhänen.

The judge asked, "What did 'Mark' say?"

"He said that we have to find couple of places to hide some money."

"How much money?"

"Five thousand dollars."

"Will you tell us what else 'Mark' said?" the prosecutor inquired.

"All he said that $5,000 we have to give to Agent Stone's wife."

"Agent Stone's wife?" clarified the prosecutor.

"Yes."

"Was 'Stone' a code name?"

"Yes, code name," said Häyhänen.

"Now, what were you to do with the money in Bear Mountain Park?"

Häyhänen replied, "'Mark' told that we have to locate 'Stone's' wife and ask her to come to Bear Mountain Park where we can talk with her and give her that money."

"Did you actually bury the money in Bear Mountain Park?"

"Yes, we did."

"Did you at any time in the future bring Helen Sobell to Bear Mountain Park?"

"No, we did not," said Häyhänen.

"Did you have a further conversation with the defendant, 'Mark,' about this money that was buried in Bear Mountain Park?"

"Yes, we had."

"Will you tell us about that conversation?"

"'Mark' told me that I got instructions to give those money to Helen Sobell."

The prosecutor asked, "Did 'Mark' say from whom he had gotten the instructions?"

"From Moscow," replied Häyhänen.

"Did 'Mark' tell you what the instructions were, in addition to giving the money to Helen Sobell?"

"To locate Helen Sobell, and 'Mark' told that he tried several times to locate her, but close to her apartment on street corner near there was almost all the time a policeman."

"Do you know whether 'Mark' was advised of her address?"

"Yes, in that message there was her address which was mentioned around 145th or 147th Street in Manhattan," said Häyhänen.

"Did 'Mark' tell you whether or not the message contained any method of identifying Helen Sobell?"

"'Mark' told me that he got a letter from the man who recruited 'Stone' as an agent. That when Helen Sobell would read that letter, she will know then that that is right man who will give that money from Soviet espionage."

"Would you tell us approximately when this conversation occurred—this Bear Mountain trip and the subsequent conversation?"

"It was springtime in 1955," replied Häyhänen.

"Just before 'Mark' went to Moscow?"

"Yes, about several weeks before."

The prosecutor asked, "Did 'Mark' tell you the name of the agent who reportedly recruited Sobell?"

"No."

"Now, did you have any further conversations with 'Mark' about Mrs. Sobell?"

"Yes, we had," said Häyhänen.

"Will you tell us about those conversations prior to 'Mark's' visit to Moscow?"

"We been talking about Helen Sobell and been driving to that street where Helen Sobell should live. And Mark showed me the house. I cannot remember now exactly the number, was it 304 or 306 or 308—one of those three numbers."

"Now, did you enter the house?" asked the prosecutor.

"No."

"After your trip with 'Mark' to Mrs. Sobell's home, did you receive an assignment from the defendant concerning Mrs. Sobell?"

"Yes," said Häyhänen.

"Will you tell us when it was?"

Häyhänen responded, "Because Mark was preparing for Moscow trip, he told that he wouldn't have enough time to locate Helen Sobell. That I have to locate her and to give that money."

"He instructed you then to give Mrs. Sobell the $5,000?"

"That is right."

"At that time where was the $5,000?" asked the prosecutor.

"They been buried in Bear Mountain Park."

"How was it buried—all together or how?"

"No, in two different places—$3,000 and $2,000," said Häyhänen.

The judge interjected, "Why not gratify our curiosity about it? Were the bills encased in anything? Were they wrapped in anything?"

"Yes, they been wrapped in cellophane bag and in paper."

The judge asked, "Who did the wrapping?"

"'Mark' did," replied Häyhänen.

The judge said, "Did you see him do it?"

Häyhänen replied, "No, I didn't see him doing it, but I saw those two packages."

The judge clarified, "In his possession?"

"Yes, and then we buried them together at Bear Mountain Park."

"Did you follow 'Mark's' instructions and give Mrs. Sobell the $5,000?" asked the prosecutor.

"No, I did not."

"Did you report what you had done in connection with Mrs. Sobell?"

"Yes, I did," Häyhänen said.

"And how did you report your action?"

"I reported that I located Helen Sobell, and I gave money and told to her to spend them carefully."

"How did you make this report? Was it to the defendant through a drop?"

Häyhänen responded, "It was through a drop to Moscow officials."

"Did you receive an answer through a drop?"

"Yes."

"What did the answer say?"

"The answer was that to locate Helen Sobell once more to talk with her once more and to decide is it possible to use her as an agent."

The prosecutor persisted. "Was there anything in the message that purported to tell anything about her prior activities?"

"When 'Mark' explained to me that money should be given to 'Stone's' wife, he explained that usually in Soviet espionage practice they recruit husband and wife together as agents," said Häyhänen.

"So is your understanding from 'Mark' that both husband and wife had been agents for the Soviet Union?"

"Yes."

"Now, is there anything contained in the message that you received concerning any future money?" the prosecutor asked.

"'Mark' explained after returning from Moscow that he got instructions to locate Helen Sobell, to give her $5,000 more."

"Did you say this is a conversation *after* he returned from Moscow?"

"Yes," said Häyhänen

"Did he say anything else after that conversation concerning Helen Sobell?"

"Yes, he did. That I have to locate her once more and that we have to arrange meeting place somewhere off Broadway, when you are driving by Saw Mill River Parkway."

The prosecutor asked, "Did you have a meeting with Helen Sobell?"

"No."

"Did you have any communication with her?

"No, but 'Mark' explained that he got those $5,000 in the bank."

The prosecutor persisted. "Now, this is *not* the same $5,000 that you buried?"

"No," reiterated Häyhänen.

"Did you have any other conversation with the defendant, 'Mark,' concerning Helen Sobell thereafter?"

"No," replied Häyhänen.

The questioning about the buried money continued the next day.

"Mr. Häyhänen, yesterday you testified that you and the defendant had buried $5,000 in Bear Mountain Park, and that the purpose was to transmit the $5,000 eventually to Mrs. Sobell. Is that correct?

"That's right."

"And you also testified you did not transmit that money, isn't that correct?"

"I did."

"Will you tell us what you did with it?"

"I kept it myself," said Häyhänen.

CHAPTER SIX

Prominent in the Abel trial was the name of Roy Rhodes, even though Abel and Rhodes never actually met one another.

Sergeant Rhodes was an American soldier working in the motor pool at the US Embassy in Moscow while Abel was in the States. Rhodes—bribed with cash and sex with an attractive Russian agent—would later become a Soviet agent for a brief time before returning to the States, and Abel was instructed to try and find Rhodes, who supposedly had relatives working in atomic weapons facilities, which the Soviets thought might be useful.

* * *

To substantiate its position that Roy Rhodes—aka 'Quebec'—was working for the Soviets, the prosecutor introduced as an exhibit in the Abel trial a piece of microfilm containing a summary of Rhodes's background:

> 'Quebec.' Roy A. Rhodes, born 1917 in Oilton, Oklahoma, U.S., Senior Sergeant of the War Ministry, former employee of the U.S. Military Attaché Staff in our country. He was a chief of the garage of the Embassy.
>
> He was recruited to our service in January 1952 in our country which he left in June 1953. Recruited on the basis of compromising materials but he is tied up to us with his receipts and information he had given in his own handwriting.

He had been trained in code work at the Ministry before he went to work at the Embassy, but as a code worker he was not used by the Embassy.

After he left our country, he was to be sent to the School of Communications of the Army C. I. Service, which is at the City of San Luis Obispo, California.

He was to be trained there as a mechanic of the coding machines.

He fully agreed to continue to cooperate with us in the States or any other country. It was agreed that he was to have written to our Embassy here special letters, but we had received none during the last year.

It has been recently learned that 'Quebec' is living in Red Bank, NJ—NJ, the abbreviation for New Jersey—where he owns three garages. The garage job is being done by his wife. His own occupation at present is not known.

His father, Mr. W. A. Rhodes, resides in the US. His brother is also in the States, where he works as an engineer at an atomic plant in Camp, Georgia, together with his brother-in-law and his father.

Clearly, Rhodes had been an important source of information for the Soviets while he was in Moscow. It was equally obvious that he had received a plea bargain of some kind from US prosecutors in order to provide his testimony to help convict Abel of espionage.

* * *

In the Abel trial, the prosecutor asked Rhodes about his assignment to Russia. "During the course of your military service, Sergeant, were you assigned to duty in the Soviet Union?"

"I was."

"And what date did you arrive in the Soviet Union?"

"May 22, 1951."

"In what part of the Soviet Union? What city?"

"Moscow."

"And was your period of duty confined to services in Moscow?"

"It was in the American Embassy."

"How long were you assigned to Moscow?" asked the prosecutor.

"I left there the last of June of 1953. Just a little over two years."

"Following your duty in Moscow, where were you assigned?"

"San Luis Obispo, California."

"During this period that you were stationed in Moscow, Sergeant, were your family present with you?"

"They were," said Rhodes.

"Did they go to Moscow with you, or did they come after?"

"They came after."

"Do you recall approximately the time that they arrived in Moscow?"

"I believe it was around the 20th of February of 1952."

"Did you make an application to the embassy to have your family join you?" asked the prosecutor.

"I did."

"Following that application, were you advised that your application had been approved?"

"I was."

"Do you recall approximately when that was, the date that you were so advised?"

"This was in December of 1951."

The prosecutor asked, "During the time that you were assigned to Moscow, in the Soviet Union, what were your duties?"

"I was motor sergeant for the embassy."

"Could you describe to the court, and to the jury generally, the location of the embassy as relates to the garage of the embassy—just the physical location?"

Rhodes replied, "The physical location of the garage that the Russians had assigned to the American embassy for the maintenance of the fleet of cars in that embassy, maintained by it, was approximately one-and-a-half miles away from the physical location of the embassy."

"When you first arrived in Moscow, where did you live?"

"In the embassy. I lived in the embassy all the time I was in Moscow."

"To whom were you assigned in the embassy?" asked the prosecutor.

"Actually to the State Department," replied Rhodes.

"Would it be that you were assigned to the military attaché?"

"My orders and my trip, and so forth, were issued by the army, but in actuality I worked for the State Department there," said Rhodes.

* * *

The prosecutor continued with his investigation of Rhodes.

"Would you tell us what happened, just briefly, on that day in December 1951? Where did you receive the news?"

"This day in question, as I can recall, I had worked in the garage in the morning, and came down to the embassy for lunch, and on arriving in the embassy I was notified by the State Department that the Russian foreign office had approved my wife's visa and that she would be joining me shortly," said Rhodes.

"What did you do after lunch?"

Rhodes replied, "During lunch I had had a few drinks—is that what you want me to bring out?"

"Well, whatever happened after lunch," said the prosecutor.

"During lunch," Rhodes replied, "I went down to the Marines. There had been a few drinks; in fact, several drinks, before I got around to going back to the garage. On arriving back to the garage, the two Russian nationals, mechanics that worked for me there in the garage, I believe, as I can recall it, that I decided that they should have a drink with me, and so one drink led to another, and apparently it went on all afternoon. At 3:30 or 4:00 in the afternoon, I suppose, something like that, the youngest mechanic's girlfriend had his car that day, and she came up to the garage to pick him up, and there was still some of the vodka left that we had been drinking that afternoon, so I said, 'Why don't you bring your girl in for a drink?' And when she came in there was a girl with her, and I had never seen the girl before. So we had a few more drinks from whatever was left of the vodka, as I can recall it, and I don't know who suggested it, that maybe we should have dinner that night, but possibly I did."

Rhodes continued, "I just can't recall exactly how it got started, but we left the garage in his car with the two girls, and I know we made a trip to, I guess it was, his apartment. I never was inside of it. I don't know what was on the inside of this building. But anyway, he was gone fifteen or twenty minutes. He cleaned up and changed his clothes, and came back to the car, and the four of us went to one of the hotels in Moscow, and the party just rolled on through the night, and I know that I was dancing, drinking, and eating with these people, and I have no recollection of leaving the hotel in any way, shape, or form. I don't know; possibly, I passed out there and they had to carry me out. I know I woke up the next morning in bed with this girl in what I had taken to be her room."

The prosecutor pressed in. "Sergeant, do you recall the name of either of the two mechanics that you mentioned that worked in the garage with you?"

Rhodes replied, "The mechanics I know well—they are Vassily and Ivan. I don't know their last names."

* * *

The prosecutor then asked, "After this evening that you mentioned, in question, did you see either of the young ladies thereafter?"

"I did," said Rhodes.

"Both of them, or just one?"

Rhodes replied, "Well, other than when this girlfriend of the mechanic's drove up to get him at the garage, which I don't remember ever talking to her after that."

The prosecutor clarified, "This would be the other girl?"

"Yes."

"Did you see her thereafter?"

Rhodes responded, "Yes, sir. As best I can recall, it would be anywhere from five to seven weeks after this party, and as I can recall it, there was this phone call to the mechanic, originally; I mean, he answered the phone there in the garage because most of the time it was some Russian who called on the phone, and he spoke a good deal of English, so he normally answered the phone. In this instance, I am sure that he answered the phone. He told me it was this girl. She wanted to talk to me."

"As a result of that phone call—or following that phone call—did you see the young lady?" the prosecutor asked.

"I did. I agreed to meet her and did meet her."

"Was she alone or was somebody with her?"

Rhodes answered, "At the time that I met her, she was by herself."

"All right. What did you do?"

"I rode the subway to the appointed place where I agreed to meet this girl. So we were walking on the street, and she was telling me that she has trouble. We walked up the street, and we were accosted by two men, two Russians I had taken them to be, nationals."

"Did one of the men speak English?" asked the prosecutor.

"One of the men spoke English."

"Do you know the names of either of these two men?"

Rhodes replied, "One of them was introduced as the girl's brother. I have no idea what his name was. The other one was introduced—the girl introduced him, I think—by a Russian name, and he said, 'Just call me 'Bob Day.'"

"'Bob Day?'"

"'Bob Smith' or 'Bob Day.' I am not positive which name was used, but I believe it was 'Bob Day.'"

The prosecutor continued. "All right. Now, after you met these two men, what did you do? Don't tell us anything about any conversation, but just exactly what did you do?"

"We went back into what I had taken to be the room I woke up in prior to this meeting, where I had been after this party," replied Rhodes.

"Did the three of you enter the room?"

Rhodes said, "The two men and myself, yes. The girl did not go in."

"What happened to the girl, do you know?"

"She walked on down the hall after we went upstairs," said Rhodes.

"Did you ever see her after that?"

"I have never seen her again."

* * *

The prosecutor continued to query Rhodes about his numerous contacts with KGB agents.

"Now, 'Bob Smith,' or the man that you think is 'Bob Smith,' and another man, and yourself, were in the room. Could you tell us what happened? Not what was said, but what happened? Did you have a conversation?"

"We had a conversation."

"Did you eat or drink anything?"

"No," replied Rhodes.

"How long did the conversation last?"

"Two hours, approximately, the best that I can figure it out. Maybe a little longer."

The prosecutor asked, "Now, did you see either of these two individuals at a later date?"

"I did."

"When did you next see them, either or both?"

Rhodes responded, "There was only one of them, the one I called 'Bob Day,' and he met me three days later, about three days later."

"The other man who was with him, at the time—whose name you don't recall—did you ever see him thereafter?"

"I never saw him again," said Rhodes.

"Can you tell us what you did at the next meeting with 'Bob Smith?'"

Rhodes replied, "At this meeting, I ate and drank and got drunk, and as to what actually happened at this meeting, I don't actually know."

"Do you remember where it took place?"

"This was in a hotel. The name I don't know."

"When did you next see 'Bob Smith,' or 'Bob Day?'"

"It would have been two or three months after that," said Rhodes.

The prosecutor asked, "And where did you see him?"

"This was in an apartment."

"And did you see him alone?"

Rhodes answered, "No. At this meeting there was, I recall, five other Russians. I had taken them to be Russians. There were two in civilian clothes and three in military uniform."

"You said that they were in military uniform? And military uniform of what nation?"

"Of Russia," replied Rhodes.

"All right. Now, will you go on and tell us what happened in that room?"

"We had a meeting," said Rhodes.

"Did you eat?" asked the prosecutor.

"I don't recall," said Rhodes. "I believe I drank a little. There was eats there if I wanted to use them."

"And how long did that meeting last?" asked the prosecutor.

"It would have been about the same time, anywhere from an hour and a half to two hours," said Rhodes.

"Sergeant, did you have meetings with these individuals whom we have just described on several occasions?" the prosecutor asked.

"I think a total of maybe fifteen times."

"Were these meetings with the same five men, two being civilians and three in military uniforms?"

Rhodes clarified: "No, sir. My meetings almost completely were with the one individual. There were only two or three times where there was more than one individual present."

"And was that individual usually the one that you knew as 'Bob Smith' or 'Bob Day?'" asked the prosecutor.

"He was the one," said Rhodes.

"In more than one of the meetings, were people present in the military uniforms that you described?" asked the prosecutor.

"There was one other meeting where there were military uniforms present, yes, sir."

"At these meetings, did you furnish any information?" asked the prosecutor.

"Yes, sir."

The prosecutor then said, "Did you at any time receive money from these individuals?"

"Yes, sir," replied Rhodes.

"Would you tell us the total amount, we will say, over the period that you were in Moscow?"

Rhodes answered, "Somewhere between $2,500 and $3,000."

"Do you recall the number of times the money was given to you?"

"Five or six times, I believe."

"Do you recall the first payment or the first sum that was given to you, Sergeant?"

"I do," replied Rhodes. "The first money I had from them, I discovered it in my clothing after I returned from Germany; I don't know whether just a day or two after I got back from Germany, going back to the meeting at the hotel with 'Bob Smith' or 'Day,' the following night. I left Moscow for Germany to get my family in Frankfurt. I was gone approximately twelve to fifteen days, total, and I got back into Moscow about the 20th of February, and sometime after that, and prior to the next meeting I had had with the Russians, I discovered I had two thousand rubles of money that I could not account for."

"What is the two thousand rubles in American money?" asked Thompkins.

"Five hundred dollars."

"And, then, is it your testimony that maybe on five or six other occasions you received money from the Russians?"

"Yes, sir."

* * *

The prosecutor resumed his examination of Rhodes, asking about the sensitive information that Rhodes provided to the Soviet government. "Now, you stated that you did give information to these people?"

"Yes, sir."

"Was your information truthful or untruthful?"

"Some of both," shrugged Rhodes.

"Did you furnish them with information with relation to your duties in the embassy?"

"Yes, sir."

"Did you furnish them with information that you had been trained in code work?"

"Yes, sir."

"Do you recall whether you furnished them with information relative to the habits of military personnel assigned to the embassy?"

"Yes, sir."

"And relative to the habits of State Department personnel?"

"Yes, sir."

"Prior to the time that you went to Moscow, Sergeant, you stated that you were in the army, as I understand it? And during the time that you were in the Pentagon, what kind of training did you receive?" the prosecutor asked.

"The time that I was in the Pentagon I received code room training, administration, and finance, I believe."

The prosecutor continued the line of questioning. "Did you furnish information to these individuals that you testified about concerning your duties at the Pentagon?" asked the prosecutor.

"Yes, sir," confirmed Rhodes.

The prosecutor delved further. "And would that include your code training while you were at the Pentagon in 1950?"

"Yes, sir."

"Sergeant, after you returned to the United States, did you have a method of communicating—by that I mean getting in touch—with the Russian Embassy in the United States?"

"I did, yes, sir," said Rhodes.

"Will you tell us about that, please?"

Rhodes explained. "On departing from Moscow, there were three systems for communicating. For me to get in communication with the Russians, I was to furnish, from the *New York Times*, any article I picked out that was critical in relation to the Russian economy, the Russian embassy, whatever you have, as long as it was critical of Russia. Three of these articles from any paper were to be lettered with a big question mark in Crayola or pencil, and sent to the Russian Embassy in Washington, DC. These were to be dispatched on any given day of the week, but the same day for three weeks running I should mail one of these critical items. On the fourth week, on the same day, I was to be in front of a theatre in Mexico City, in Old Mexico, in contact with whoever they designated to meet me."

"Did you have any knowledge of how you were to be dressed?"

"There was no particular dress," Rhodes said, "but I was to be carrying or smoking a pipe that they furnished me."

The prosecutor continued, "After you came back to the United States, did you try to communicate with the Russian embassy?"

"No, sir."

"Did you try and communicate with anybody in this country?"

"No, sir," replied Rhodes.

"No further questions, your Honor," the prosecutor stated.

* * *

In its opinion affirming the conviction of Abel, the appellate court described the importance of Häyhänen's testimony concerning Roy Rhodes:

> *To be sure, Abel was not chargeable with responsibility for Rhodes's activities while the latter was in Moscow; but the fact that Rhodes had engaged in those activities, that he had notified Soviet agents of his transfer to the United States, and that arrangements were made whereby Rhodes and Soviet agents could contact one another in this country, lent credence to the testimony of Häyhänen that he and Abel, both agents of the Soviet government, had received instructions to locate Rhodes and that they had made efforts to do so.*

The court continued:

> *Phrased somewhat differently, the effect of Rhodes's testimony was to better enable the jury to pass upon the credibility of a material portion of the testimony of Häyhänen. The jury determination as to whether Häyhänen spoke truthfully or falsely about the instructions he had received and the efforts made by him and Abel to locate Rhodes was materially aided by testimony tending to show that a strong motive existed to locate the latter. Rhodes's testimony provided the motive.*

The activities of Roy Rhodes would become a critical part of the prosecutor's case against Rudolf Abel.

CHAPTER SEVEN

After five years in the states, Reino Häyhänen had finally had enough of the spy business, and in early May of 1957, he defected at the American Embassy in Paris while he was on vacation in Europe. His light brown hair had been dyed jet black, and underneath his fedora was a large, dark pair of sunglasses to hide his gray-blue eyes.

At Abel's trial, Häyhänen described meeting Rudolf Abel at Prospect Park to arrange Häyhänen's travel to Russia.

The prosecutor asked, "How was that meeting set up? Was it through a message?"

"Yes. I left a message in signal place for 'Mark,'" said Häyhänen. "I put number—I cannot remember exactly number—which was I think it was six. It meant sixteenth of February have to meet."

"When you arrived at the meeting place on that date, did you see 'Mark?'" asked the prosecutor.

"Yes, I saw him."

"Where was he?"

Häyhänen replied, "He was hiding behind bushes and he was checking that nobody was following me."

"In connection with your travel to Europe, did you receive any further instructions from the defendant?" asked the prosecutor.

"Like I mentioned before, I got those instructions how to make that phone call in Paris. 'Mark' explained how to use those Paris phones, because they are a little bit different than in New York City—different way of calling."

"Now, just a little while ago you testified that you sent 'Mark' a message concerning the *Queen Elizabeth*. Is that correct?"

"Yes."

"Now, you finally decided to go to Europe?"

"Yes," replied Häyhänen.

"By way of ship to Paris, is that correct?"

"That's right. The ship to Le Havre."

"Did you advise anybody of your departure?" asked the prosecutor.

"Yes, I did. I sent a message to Soviet officials through drop number three, Fort Tryon Park."

"And what did you advise them?"

Häyhänen said, "I sent a message that I am leaving New York City 24th of April, 1957, on the ship *Liberté*."

"Now, did you board the ship on April 24, 1957?"

"Yes, I did."

"Did you arrive at Le Havre?" the prosecutor asked.

"Yes, I did. And next day I arrived to Paris."

The prosecutor continued, "You mentioned that you had received instructions from 'Mark' in New York about what to do in Paris—is that correct?"

"That is right."

"What did you do pursuant to his instructions?"

Häyhänen responded, "I called in Paris by the phone KLE-3341, for my best recollection, was the phone number."

"All right, and what happened?"

"And then in Russian, I asked the passwords, 'Can I send through your office two parcels to the USSR, without Mori Company?' And I got an answer."

The prosecutor asked, "As a result of that reply, what did you do?"

"I went to meeting place, and I met one Russian official."

"What were you wearing?"

"I was wearing the blue tie and was smoking a pipe," said Häyhänen.

"Now, when you met the Russian official, what did you say, if you recall?"

Häyhänen replied, "He said passwords, but I cannot recall now which they were. But he told that he recognized me at once by the way I was smoking the pipe, and I had that blue tie with red stripes."

"You had a blue tie with red stripes on, and you were smoking a pipe?"

"That's right."

"Did someone approach you?" asked the prosecutor.

"Yes."

The judge inquired, "You spoke with him? You had a conversation with him?"

"Yes, I was talking to that Russian official."

The judge then asked, "In what language did you converse with him?"

"In Russian."

The prosecutor asked, "How was this person dressed, if you remember?"

"He was dressed in brown overcoat, then brown hat, gray suit."

"Now, as a result of this meeting, what did you do next?" asked the prosecutor.

"We been walking several blocks, and then we went to one bar where we been drinking cognac and had a cup of coffee."

"Now, what happened after that?"

"Then he gave me some money in French francs and in American dollars—$200," said Häyhänen.

"Did you meet anyone the next day?"

"I met him next night just for visual meeting. And it was agreed the previous day that if I won't wear a hat and I have any magazine or newspaper in my hand—that it means that I am leaving next day then."

"Leaving next day for where?" asked the prosecutor.

Häyhänen said, "For West Germany, and from there then by the plane to West Berlin."

"Did you see him thereafter?"

"No, I did not."

"The next day, where did you go?" asked the prosecutor.

"The next day, I went then to American legation in Paris."

* * *

After Häyhänen walked into the American Embassy in Paris, he told the ambassador that he was traveling on a fake US passport that bore the name of Eugene Nicolai Maki and that, while he was a KGB agent, he had transmitted reams of top secret US Military data to Moscow. The embassy then arranged to have Häyhänen flown to Washington, where he could be further interrogated by the FBI. At that point, Rudolf Abel was none the wiser.

The prosecutor in Abel's trial asked Häyhänen about the details of his defection.

"After you went to the embassy, what did you do?"

"I explained that I am Russian espionage officer in rank of lieutenant colonel, and I have some information what I like to give to American officials to help."

The prosecutor asked, "At the time that you went in the American Embassy and conferred with these officials, did you give them anything?"

"Yes, I gave as proof Finnish five marks coin which I explained is a container that is made from two coins," said Häyhänen.

"Is there any particular reason why you can identify that coin?"

"There is hole—if you punch with needle, you can open this container."

"On the times that you went to the American Embassy, did you have conversations with American officials?" the prosecutor asked.

"Yes, I had."

"And did you tell them of your activities in the United States?" Häyhänen replied, "Yes, I did."

"Did you return to the United States?"

"Yes, I did."

"Do you recall roughly the date that you got back to the United States?"

Häyhänen responded, "I believe it was the 11th of May, 1957," Häyhänen said.

The prosecutor asked, "Subsequent to your return to the United States, have you received any financial assistance from the United States government?"

"Yes, I did."

"Did you meet with representatives of the FBI?"

"Yes, I did."

"Did you tell them about your activities?" asked the prosecutor.

"Yes, I did."

"Did you tell the FBI about your drops?"

"Yes, I did," replied Häyhänen.

"Did you give the FBI permission to search your home?"

"Yes, I did."

"And did you give them a sketch of your home?"

"Yes, I did."

* * *

With the information Häyhänen provided to the FBI, his home in Peekskill, New York, was thoroughly searched for evidence verifying his claims to be a Soviet operative. In Abel's trial, the government called FBI agent Edward F. Gamber as a witness to describe the details of the search of Häyhänen's home and what was found there.

"Mr. Gamber, would you state your occupation, please?" asked the prosecutor.

"I am a special agent in the Federal Bureau of Investigation."

"Directing your attention to May 12th of this year, do you recall where you were on that date?" the prosecutor asked.

"In Peekskill, New York."

"In the course of your official duties, did you on that date have occasion to search the premises of one Reino Häyhänen?"

"I did," replied Gamber.

"Did you know Mr. Häyhänen by any other name?"

"I did. I knew him by the name of 'Eugene N. Maki.'"

"You say that you did have occasion to conduct a search of his home?"

"I did."

"Were there any other special agents with you during the search?"

"There were. Special Agents John T. Mullhern and George M. Massett were present, and they participated," replied Gamber.

"So that the three of you conducted the search of his home?"

"That is right, Special Agents John G. Willis, Douglas P. White, Eugene Oja, and Special Employee Kenneth E. Delanoi were also present."

"Was either Mr. or Mrs. Maki present during the conduct of the search?"

"Mrs. Maki was present," said Gamber.

"Will you tell us the duration of the search on that day, May 12th?"

"The search commenced at approximately 4:30 p.m. and continued until approximately 11:05 p.m."

"I show you what has been marked as Government's Exhibit 40 for identification and ask if you can identify that?"

"This is a diagram which we used in searching Reino Häyhänen's home," confirmed Gamber.

"Can you tell us from whom the FBI had secured that diagram?"

"This diagram was received from Reino Häyhänen."

"Did you use that diagram in any way in conducting your search?"

Gamber responded, "Yes, we used this diagram in our search of the cellar of Reino Häyhänen's home."

"And in connection with your search of the cellar, and the use of the diagram, were you searching for any specific object?"

"We were searching for a birth certificate which was buried in the cellar of the home, that is designated by an 'X' on that diagram."

"Will you explain to the court and jury how you made use of that diagram in the conduct of your search?" asked the prosecutor.

"That diagram contains an 'X' between two marks which indicate the supporting pillars in the rear of the basement of Reino Häyhänen's home. By use of that diagram, we located a spot directly between these two supporting posts and began to dig there to locate this birth certificate."

"And did you locate anything?" the prosecutor inquired.

Gamber replied, "Yes; a distance of fifty-three inches from the left supporting post, and forty-one inches from the right supporting post, we located a package buried approximately five inches in the sand."

"Now, Mr. Gamber, at the time of conducting a search of Mr. Häyhänen's home on this evening, did you also seize a radio?"

"Yes, I seized a radio which was located under a table in the living room of Reino Häyhänen's home."

"Mr. Gamber, during the course of your search did you also seize some photographic equipment?

"Yes, we did. We seized some photographic paper, both in a roll form and in a flat form. We seized some photographic chemicals. We seized some trays and beakers used in processing film. We seized some frames for drying film. We seized some hangers for drying film. We seized an enlarger and a number of other photographic articles which I do not specifically recall at this time," replied Gamber.

"No further questions, your Honor," said the prosecutor.

* * *

As it turned out, Reino Häyhänen was extremely useful to US authorities, and he was able to help them solve several mysteries that had perplexed them for years. In particular, the FBI had years before found a hollowed-out bolt in one of the "dead drops" mentioned by Häyhänen—a hole in a set of cement steps in Prospect Park. The bolt was about two inches long and one-fourth inch in diameter. It contained the following typewritten message:

Nobody came to meeting either 8 or 9th. . .as I was advised he should. Why? Should he be inside or outside? Is time wrong? Place seems right. Please check.

Apparently, one of the drops Häyhänen used had contained a US five-cent piece hollowed out to serve as a concealment for microfilm or miniature code pads. Before the often-careless Häyhänen had a chance to open the nickel, he absentmindedly spent it. The coin circulated in the New York economy for seven months before a newsboy dropped it and it broke open, revealing a tiny sheet of number groups. The hollow nickel case remained unsolved for four years, because investigators were unable to decipher the coded message inside.

Häyhänen confirmed that containers such as this were often used for communications between Soviet spies. Among the items he had been supplied by the Soviets were hollow pens, pencils, screws, batteries, and coins for transporting messages. In Häyhänen's home, FBI agents found such items, including a fifty-markka coin from Finland. It had been hollowed out, and there was a small hole in the first "a" of the word "Tasavalta" on the coin. FBI lab experts examined the coin, and they immediately noted that it bore a great similarity to the Jefferson nickel that a Brooklyn newsboy had discovered in 1953.

The story went like this: on the evening of Monday, June 22, 1953, a delivery boy for the *Brooklyn Eagle* knocked on the door of one of his customers to collect money for the paper. One of the coins felt considerably lighter than the others, and when the young boy dropped the coin to the floor, it fell apart. Inside was a tiny photograph which appeared to include a series of numbers. Two days later, a detective of the New York City Police Department mentioned to an FBI agent that he had heard of a strange hollow nickel which had been discovered by a Brooklyn youth.

The New York detective contacted the boy, who handed over the hollow nickel and the photograph it contained. In examining the nickel, agents of the FBI noted that the micro-photograph appeared to portray ten columns of typewritten numbers. The agents immediately suspected that they had found a coded espionage message, but they were unable to decipher it.

The newspaper boy, James Bozart, was later called to testify in the Abel trial by the prosecution.

"How old are you?" asked the prosecutor.

Bozart replied, "Seventeen and a half."

"Directing your attention to the summer of 1953, were you at that time a newspaper delivery boy?"

"Yes, I was."

"And specifically directing your attention to an occasion in the summer of 1953, when you were making collections during your route, do you recall a specific incident at which time you were given fifty cents in change at 3403 Foster Avenue in Brooklyn?"

Bozart replied, "Yes, I do."

"Now, what was the change that you received on that occasion?" asked the prosecutor.

"A quarter and five nickels."

"After receiving the change, would you tell us what happened?"

"Well, I left the apartment door," Bozart said, "and I was walking down the stairs. You see, it's in an apartment building. And the change slipped from my hand and it dropped on the staircase. And when I picked it up, one of the nickels was split in half."

"And you picked up the two pieces, did you?"

"Yes, I did."

"Was there anything in either of the pieces?"

Bozart responded, "One of them—half of the nickel—had a piece of microfilm in it."

"Did you look at the piece of microfilm?" the prosecutor asked.

"Yes, I did."

"Was there anything on it?"

Bozart replied, "Yes. It was a picture of a file card, or an index card."

"Could you state whether there was any writing or printing or anything on it?"

"On the file card?" asked Bozart for clarification.

"On the microfilm," replied the prosecutor.

Bozart said, "Yes. Oh, it had a picture of a file card and on the file card there seemed to be rows of numbers."

* * *

The FBI extensively interviewed Häyhänen about the codes and cryptosystems which he had used in the Soviet intelligence agencies he had served. The information which he provided was applied by FBI laboratory experts to the micro-photograph from the Jefferson nickel found by the newspaper boy. With this data, the FBI laboratory succeeded in breaking through the shroud of mystery surrounding the coded message.

The message apparently was intended for Häyhänen and had been sent from the Soviet Union shortly after his arrival in the United States. It read:

1. We congratulate you on a safe arrival. We confirm the receipt of your letter.

2. We gave instructions to transmit to you three thousand in local currency. Consult with us prior to investing it in any kind of business, first advising us of the character of the business.

3. According to your request, we will transmit the formula for the preparation of soft film, along with your mother's letter.

4. It is too early to send you the gammas. Encipher short letter. All the data about yourself, place of work, address, etc. must not be transmitted in one cipher message.

5. The package was delivered to your wife personally. Everything is all right with the family. We wish you success. Greeting from the comrades.

* * *

In the Abel trial, another special agent of the FBI who worked as a document examiner in its Washington, DC lab, was called to the stand to explain microdots.

"Would you explain to the jury what a microdot is?" asked the prosecutor.

"A microdot is the term ordinarily used for a photograph reduction made of a document," Frederick Webb replied. "The document could be one—the size of the tablet sheet here, eight by ten inches, or something of that kind—reduced down to a size about the size of a period on a typewriter."

The agent continued, "Or it might even be a little smaller or a little larger, but that would be the order of what is commonly referred to as a microdot. The original sheet may have a type-written message—it could even have a handwritten message or drawing and, when reduced to that size, would be capable of being enlarged in a manner so that it would be readable."

The prosecutor then asked, "Now, would you explain how the sheet containing writing or a diagram or whatever it might be—what process would be followed to reduce that to a small size such as you have indicated?"

"Well, one very usual process would be to perhaps make a two-step reduction," said Webb. "First, produce a negative with a thirty-five-millimeter camera and then take that reduced negative, and in a second step—with a very short focal length lens and using light transmitted through this thirty-five-millimeter negative—produce along a suitable photographic material an exposure at this reduced microdot size."

"Now, in that process of reduction, is there a special type of film that is necessary?" inquired the prosecutor.

"You would have to use a type of film which would record the image accurately at that reduction, and some kinds of photographic materials are not suitable because the grain of emulsion is too coarse, and they will not resolve the lines at that great reduction."

The prosecutor said, "I show you what has been marked as Government's Exhibit Number 27 in evidence, which is a box of film, spectroscopic film, and I will ask you if you are familiar with spectroscopic film of that type?"

"Yes, sir."

"Are you familiar with the qualities of that film?"

"Yes, sir."

"Would you explain what those qualities are?"

The agent responded, "Well, the principal quality with reference to microdot work is that this film is capable of producing an image that would be, that you would make under the reduction that you would attempt to get in a microdot. In other words, this film is capable of recording about 1,000 lines per millimeter, which means that it has extreme resolving power, and therefore the blacks in the image that you would get under microdot reductions would be recorded separate from the white portions."

The agent resumed. "So that there would be a separation from one part of the letter to the other, in the typewritten message, say, or from one letter to the next, which would make it possible to examine the microdot through a microscope and read it or to photographically enlarge it and get a picture of it that would be readable."

"Is that a high-emulsion film?" asked the prosecutor.

"A film with high resolving power. This film has an emulsion especially prepared so that it has a high resolving power, which ordinarily is necessary in a lot of scientific work, but also makes it a good one to use if you are preparing to make a copy under extreme reductions that you would have in making a microdot."

"What do you mean by 'high resolving power?'" the prosecutor asked.

Webb replied, "High resolving power is the quality of film, well—and it is best to explain it this way: if you were to put in a millimeter a thousand separate and distinct black lines, each having a white space between them—that line and the next—this film is capable of recording those lines just as they are—with the separation of the black and the white—between them."

"And is it by reason of that quality that this film is adaptable for use in the production of microdots?" asked the prosecutor.

"Yes, sir, it is."

"What would happen, Mr. Webb, if you used a film of lower resolving power?"

"Well, if you were to attempt to do this with just ordinary photographic materials, when you tried to make a microdot at this reduction you would end up with simply a black dot and nothing when you looked through a microscope. You would not be able to see the letters or parts of the letters separated one from the other. There would be no separation of the whites. You would not be able to record it as a microdot."

"With respect to exhibit number ninety-four, being two tie clasps, would you state the results of your examination of those two tie clasps?"

Webb said, "I found that these two tie clasps open up and have cavities inside. The one which has a cylindrical-shaped ornament on the front, and the end of the cylindrical ornament comes out and reveals inside a space or a cavity. The other one, the other tie clasp which is a part of exhibit number ninety-four, has a bar, a silver bar-shaped ornament, and the front of the bar comes off and inside there is a rectangular-shaped cavity."

* * *

Reino Häyhänen had thus assisted the FBI in cracking the mystery of the hollow nickel. But the more important identities of 'Mikhail' and 'Mark' were still unsolved. For some reason, Häyhänen had the idea that 'Mikhail' was a Soviet diplomatic official and was possibly attached to the embassy or the United Nations. He described 'Mikhail' as between forty and fifty years old, of medium build with a long, thin nose and dark hair, and about five feet, nine inches tall.

This description was then compared to descriptions of Soviet representatives who had been in the United States between 1952 and 1954. From the long list of possible suspects, the most logical candidate appeared to be Mikhail Nikolaevich Svirin, who, from the latter part of August 1952 until April 1954, had served as the first secretary to the Soviet United Nations delegation in New York.

On May 16, 1957, FBI agents showed a group of photographs to Häyhänen. The moment Häyhänen's eyes fell on those of Mikhail Nikolaevich Svirin, he shouted, "That's the one! There is absolutely no doubt about it. That's 'Mikhail!'"

Unfortunately, Svirin had returned to the Soviet Union in October of 1956 and was beyond the long arm of American justice.

The FBI's next task was to identify 'Mark'. Häyhänen did not know where 'Mark' was residing or the name he was using, but Häyhänen was able to furnish other details: 'Mark' was a colonel in the KGB, had been engaged in espionage work since approximately 1927, and had come to the United States in 1948 or 1949, entering by illegally crossing the Canadian border. In keeping with instructions he received from Soviet officials, Häyhänen was first met by 'Mark' at a movie theater in Flushing, Long Island, during the late summer of 1954. For purposes of identification, Häyhänen wore a blue-and-red-striped tie and smoked a pipe.

After their introduction, Häyhänen and 'Mark' held frequent meetings in Prospect Park, on crowded streets, and in other inconspicuous places throughout New York. They also made several short trips together to Atlantic City, Philadelphia, Albany, Greenwich, and other eastern cities.

Häyhänen led the FBI to the art studio where Abel had taken Häyhänen shortly after the two started working together.

Immediately after Häyhänen's disclosure of Abel's address to US officials, FBI agents placed Abel's art studio in Brooklyn under round-the-clock surveillance by renting an apartment across the street. After that, FBI agents saw Abel go to his room at the Hotel Latham in Manhattan every night. The FBI rented a small room in the hotel immediately adjacent to Abel's so they could monitor his activities.

Meanwhile, Häyhänen continued to cooperate fully with US officials. Surprisingly, Abel was apparently none the wiser as his former colleague Häyhänen provided to the FBI a steady stream of evidence which would later be used to convict Abel for his activities as a Soviet spook.

* * *

Surveillance of Abel's art studio in Brooklyn began in earnest. The FBI rented an apartment across the street seven stories above Abel's apartment for a better perspective. In the trial of Abel, the government called as a witness Neil D. Heiner, an FBI agent who was duly sworn and who testified about seeing Abel at the apartment.

"Mr. Heiner, by whom are you employed?" asked the prosecutor.

"I am a special agent in the Federal Bureau of Investigation."

"Directing your attention to May 23, 1957, were you in the vicinity of 252 Fulton Street, Brooklyn, pursuant to your duties?"

"Yes, sir, I was."

"Will you tell the court and jury where you were?"

"I was in a position where I could observe the windows of studio or suite 505 at 252 Fulton Street," said Heiner.

"Where was your observation post with relation to those windows? Was it above?"

"It was some distance above," responded Heiner. "I was on the twelfth floor of Hotel Touraine, and these windows are on the fifth floor of the building at 252 Fulton Street."

"And you were keeping those windows under continual observation?" asked the prosecutor.

"Yes, sir."

"Will you tell us what you saw, if anything?"

Heiner replied, "Well, on the evening of May 23rd at about 10:45 p.m., I was watching the studio, and I saw one light was turned on in the studio. And I could see a male figure moving around in the room. From time to time it would pass in back of this light. There was a light suspended on a cord from the ceiling with a shield around it. I could see that this man, he was unidentified, was middle-aged and was baldheaded. He had a fringe of gray hair around the edges. He was wearing glasses. And, as I said before, he showed himself only momentarily."

Heiner continued, "My view of the entire room was obstructed except when he stood in front of the window. The lights remained on, and at about one minute before midnight I saw this man, in back of the light, put on a dark brown or dark gray summer straw hat, and it had a very bright white band. The band stood out. And then, about a minute later, the single light went out."

"Could you describe his clothing at all?" the prosecutor asked.

"Yes, I could see that he had on a short-sleeved shirt," said Heiner, "It hit him about, oh, an inch above the elbow. It seemed to be light-colored blue. He was wearing a tie. It was darker-colored. I couldn't distinguish which color. And, as I said before, he was wearing glasses. I couldn't see his entire face because his head was down. In other words, he wasn't looking out the window so I could have a full-front view of his face."

"Did I understand you to say about midnight the light went out?"

"Yes, sir."

The prosecutor then asked, "What did you do after the light went out?"

"I had radio communications with other agent personnel who were on the street in the area surrounding the studio. When the light went out, I alerted the agent personnel in the street, told them that the lights had gone out. And this information was given to them," Heiner said.

"Did you thereafter see this unidentified individual?"

"No, sir. Not that night," replied Heiner.

"Now, directing your attention to June 13, 1957, were you in the vicinity of 252 Fulton Street pursuant to your duties as a special agent of the Federal Bureau of Investigation?"

"Yes, sir. I was in the same position."

"Can you tell us what you saw?"

Heiner replied, "About 10:00 on the night of June 13th, I observed the light in the studio go on again and the same individual was seen in the room. Again, I saw him only momentarily as he passed in back of the light. The same light was on, and at 11:50 p.m., I observed this man putting on a hat very similar to the one I had seen on the previous night of May 23rd. He put this hat on, and about a minute later, the light was turned out."

Heiner continued, "And then at 11:54 p.m., walking toward my position—that would be southeast from 252 Fulton Street—an individual approached me, and he was wearing a hat similar to the one I had observed on the unidentified man in Room 505 of 252 Fulton Street."

The prosecutor asked, "Did you see him come out of 252 Fulton Street or, if you didn't, where did you first see him?"

"No, sir," said Heiner, "My view of the main entrance to 252 Fulton Street was obstructed. I actually couldn't see the front door. However, at a point at most thirty to forty feet southeast from the main entrance, I could see people walking on Fulton Street, and that is at the point I observed him."

"From the description you have given of this individual in the room and this, would you say it was the same individual?"

"Yes, sir," confirmed Heiner.

"Did you do anything after the individual passed from your view walking along Fulton Street?"

Heiner replied, "Well, when that light went out I, again, notified agent personnel and observed these agents commence to conduct surveillance of this unknown man."

"That is all you saw?"

"Yes, sir. The unidentified man passed beneath, directly beneath, me and I could see no more."

"Were you using binoculars?"

"Yes, sir."

"Will you tell us the type?"

"Well, they were ten-fifties. That means they have a power of ten magnification, and the fifty designates the millimeter width across the front of the lens. In other words, the front lenses of the binoculars were fifty millimeters wide."

"And you were using binoculars on your observation through the windows?" asked the prosecutor.

"Yes."

"And, again, when he walked along the street?"

"Yes," replied Heiner.

The FBI vantage point for the surveillance of Abel's studio happened to be right across the street from the courthouse, and the judge said to the jury, "It may help you understand the testimony. When court adjourns today, you can look out the window."

* * *

On June 13, 1957, with the surveillance data of Abel in hand, the FBI informed the INS that the FBI had information concerning an alien living illegally in this country. Sam Papich, the FBI liaison officer, contacted Mario Noto, the INS deputy assistant commissioner for special investigations. Papich also told Noto that there was substantial evidence that Abel was a Soviet spy. Interestingly enough, Noto was so focused on the immigration issue that he never asked about Abel's espionage activities.

Furthermore, Papich never suggested that INS treat the case in any particular way, and no special arrangements were made between the two agencies. Papich soon provided Noto with the information he requested—that Abel had entered the country by way of Canada, that he had used a false birth certificate, and that he had confided to several people that he was in this country illegally. Noto was also told that Abel was an officer in the KGB.

Noto again met with the FBI, and he told them the INS would promptly order the arrest of Abel for failing to notify the US Attorney General, as required by the Immigration and Nationality Act. INS officials agreed the evidence was sufficient to justify issuance of a show cause order as to Abel's deportability. It was decided that Abel should be arrested for a deportation hearing, rather than a criminal espionage offense. The show cause order and arrest warrant were prepared in Washington, DC, and Noto instructed two INS agents to apprehend Abel in New York. The FBI requested that they be able to talk with Abel before his arrest in order to determine whether Abel would agree to voluntarily "cooperate."

* * *

On June 18th and 19th, 1957, two attorneys of the Internal Security Division interviewed Reino Häyhänen as the principal witness in this matter. Although Häyhänen had furnished counterespionage information—and was willing to do so on a confidential basis—he absolutely refused to agree to testify in public for fear of reprisals taken by the USSR against his mother, brothers, and sister, who were in the Soviet Union.

Because of Häyhänen's refusal to testify—and the fact that, if he was indicted as a co-conspirator, he could invoke his privileges under the Fifth Amendment—the Internal Security Division concluded that the evidence was insufficient to secure a warrant on complaint or an indictment on charges of conspiracy to violate the espionage statutes. Had Häyhänen been willing to testify, the Internal Security Division and the FBI were prepared to take the necessary legal steps to secure a warrant and arrest Abel on espionage charges.

Therefore, the Department of Justice was unable to proceed under the espionage statutes, but could proceed under the immigration laws. Abel would then be arrested under an alien warrant and served with an order to show cause duly issued by the acting district director of the Immigration and Naturalization Service in New York City.

CHAPTER EIGHT

At 7:00 a.m. on June 21st, FBI agents broke into Abel's hotel room while INS agents waited nearby. The FBI informed Abel that they were charged with investigating matters relating to the internal security of the United States. Abel was interrogated, and he refused to answer any of the questions leveled against him. He was told that the FBI was aware he had engaged in espionage, and that if he refused to cooperate, he would be arrested before he left the room.

After half an hour of questioning, the FBI agents decided to have the INS arrest Abel. One of the INS agents later executed an affidavit describing what he found in his search of Abel's possessions:

That immediately following the service of the warrant of arrest, I went to the clothes closet in Collins room and started to search his effects which were contained therein. That during this search, in a valise he observed a wallet and thereupon he searched the same. That among the items which I found in the wallet were several slips of paper, two being typewritten and one handwritten.

That the handwritten note made reference to a symbol appearing on a pole opposite an address and set forth the time and place of a meeting. That one of the typewritten notes contained a question relating to a picture and a response relating to a pipe and book. That the other typewritten note contained the names of two individuals having addresses in the USSR.

That among Collins effects was a clothing store bill in the name of Mr. Goldfus. That he then asked Collins who Goldfus was, and Collins replied: "That's me." That included in the effects in the closet was a camera bag which, when opened, contained a camera, numerous lenses, and other photographic equipment, such as film.

That all of the said effects seized in Collins room were displayed to Special Agents of the Federal Bureau of Investigation and transported to Immigration and Naturalization Headquarters, New York City.

That he observed on a small table beside the bed, a Hallicrafters radio having a gray metal cabinet and shortwave band. That this radio was equipped with an aerial which ran up the wall of the room, across the ceiling, into the bedroom, and out the bedroom window.

After Abel's arrest, the INS agents handed him a notice of hearing for his deportation:

To: Martin Collins, Hotel Latham, 4 E. 28th St., New York, N.Y.

It appearing that you are in the United States in violation of law in that:

1. You are not a citizen or national of the United States.

2. You are a native of Russia and a national of the Union of Soviet Socialist Republics.

3. You last entered the United States at an unknown point across the boundary from Canada in 1949.

4. You failed to notify the Attorney General of your address during January 1956 and during January 1957.

5. You did not furnish notice of your address because you feared that by so doing you would disclose your illegal presence in the United States; and that you are subject to be taken into custody and deported pursuant to the following provision(s) of law: Section 241(a)(5) of the Immigration and Nationality Act, in that, you have failed to furnish notification of your address in compliance with the provisions of Section 265 and have not established that such failure was reasonably excusable or was not willful.

IT IS ORDERED, That you appear for hearing before a Special Inquiry Officer of the Immigration and Naturalization Service of the United States Department of Justice at 70 Columbus Ave., New York, N.Y. on July 1, 1957 at 2 p.m. and show cause why you should not be deported from the United States on the charge(s) set forth above.

IMMIGRATION AND NATURALIZATION SERVICE

John L. Muff
Acting District Director
New York, N.Y.
Dated: June 20, 1957

* * *

After the INS agents arrested Abel, they thoroughly searched his room for weapons and evidence of alienage. The FBI agents were present when the search was made, but they did not participate in it. The primary articles seized in this regard were: (1) a birth certificate in the name of "Martin Collins," (2) a birth certificate in the name of "Emil Goldfus," (3) an international certificate of vaccination issued in the name of "Martin Collins," and (4) a bank book issued by the East River Savings Bank in the name of "E. R. Goldfus."

While they were in Abel's room, the INS agents also seized three slips of paper. The agents told Abel that he could take with him anything he wanted, and when he finished packing, he asked for permission to repack one of his bags. While he was doing so, one of the INS agents noticed he was trying to conceal some papers in his sleeve, and these were quickly seized. One of the documents was a strip of graph paper containing a coded message in grouped digits.

At approximately 8:30 a.m., the INS agents left the hotel with Abel and drove to the district office of the INS. As soon as they left, FBI agents received written consent to search the room. These agents seized the contents of a wastebasket which contained several articles that Abel had discarded while packing. Two of the items were later admitted into evidence in Abel's trial: a piece of wood wrapped in sandpaper and containing a cipher pad, and a hollowed-out wooden pencil containing microfilm. These items were clearly incriminating—who but a spy would have them?

The inventory of the items found inside Abel's hotel room was carefully compiled by the government. This was an important task, because the federal prosecutor would have to rely on it at trial to show circumstantial evidence of Abel's activities. The list would speak for itself to reveal that Abel was clearly a Russian spy.

The extremely detailed lists that were compiled by the government read like a novel. The most striking feature was the incredible amount of espionage paraphernalia that Abel had accumulated. It was obvious that Abel had been a very busy man.

* * *

At the end of their interrogation, the INS agents handcuffed Abel and took him downtown to be booked, fingerprinted, and photographed. Abel was then taken to an airport near Newark, New Jersey, where at 4:15 p.m., he and two immigration officers boarded a small aircraft bound for McAllen, Texas, by way of Mobile, Alabama. Shortly after takeoff from Mobile, Abel was allowed to sleep on a sofa couch in the airplane. He did not awaken until 4:30 a.m., when the plane landed at Brownsville. He was then transported by automobile to McAllen, Texas, where he arrived at 5:30 a.m. and was directed to his sleeping quarters, which were private accommodations with toilet and bathing facilities separate from the other inmates. Abel was also given his choice of food, unlike the other inmates who were fed a standard daily diet.

Abel was questioned for three days by teams of INS and FBI agents. He was asked by immigration officials whether he fully understood the order to show cause which was served upon him at the Hotel Latham, a copy of which he possessed at all times, and he replied "yes." He was told that he had the right to an attorney, but he requested no assistance.

On the fourth day, he decided to admit that his real name was Rudolf Ivanovich Abel, and that he was a Russian citizen traveling on a fake US passport after illegally entering the states through Canada in 1948. At 2:10 p.m., Abel was again reminded by immigration officials that he could have any attorney of his choice or could communicate with anyone. He said he did not know any lawyers except one named "Abt" or "Apt," who was in New York City. He first stated he intended to write John Jacob Apt, the general counsel of the Communist Party USA, but changed his mind, saying he doubted that the attorney would come to Texas. Petitioner was then given a classified phone directory containing the names of all the attorneys in the area surrounding McAllen, from which he selected the law firm of Stafford, Atlas & Spilman of McAllen. At 3:45 p.m., Abel conferred for about thirty minutes with an attorney from the firm, who tentatively agreed to represent him.

The next morning at 9:40 a.m., Abel was notified that he had a right to an immediate hearing on the deportation charge instead of waiting for a thirty-day delay. Abel said he had no objection to an immediate hearing, but would be bound by what his attorney advised. Abel's attorneys were notified, and they agreed to an immediate hearing. At 3:00 p.m., Abel's attorneys conferred with him for about forty-five minutes, and they agreed that a hearing should be scheduled for the 27th day of June. A hearing was held on this date, and Abel again admitted his true identity was Rudolf Ivanovich Abel; that he was a national of Russia; that he had used the aliases of "Emil Goldfus" and "Martin Collins;" and that he was a deportable alien. When asked to designate the country to which he wished to be deported, he replied "the USSR."

The transcript of the INS hearing held on June 27, 1957, in the alien detention center revealed the following:

Date: June 27, 1957
Time: 10:00 a.m.

Respondent: Rudolf Ivanovich Abel, alias Martin Collins, alias Emil R. Goldfus

Respondent's counsel: Morris Atlas, Attorney at Law, Counsel; Robert Schwarz, Attorney at Law, Associate Counsel, of the firm Stafford, Atlas & Spilman, McAllen, Texas

Q. *I have before me an order to show cause and notice of hearing dated June 20, 1957, addressed to Martin Collins at Hotel Latham, New York, New York, which indicates that it was served in person on June 21, 1957. Were you served with a copy of this order to show cause?*

A. *Yes, sir.*

Q. *What is your true and correct name?*

A. *My true and correct name is Rudolf Ivanovich Abel.*

Q. *Have you also been known as 'Martin Collins' or 'Emil R. Goldfus?'*

A. *I have.*

Q. *Now, this order to show cause and notice of hearing indicates that you have requested that a prompt hearing be held in your case and that you have waived your right to any additional time. Is that correct, and is that your desire?*

A. *Yes, sir.*

Q. *Now, I have here also a warrant of arrest dated June 20, 1957, charging that Martin Collins, alias Emil R. Goldfus,* appears to be in the United States in violation of the immigration laws, and this warrant of arrest indicates it was served on you June 21, 1957, at 7:30 a.m.

Q. Did you receive a copy of the warrant of arrest?

A. I did.

Q. Mr. Goldfus, the order to show cause and notice of hearing alleges first you are not a citizen or national of the United States. Do you admit or do you deny that allegation?

A. I admit it.

Q. The second allegation, you are a native of Russia and a national of the Union of Soviet Socialist Republics. Do you admit that allegation is true, or do you deny it?

A. I admit it.

Q. The third allegation, you last entered the United States at an unknown point across the boundary from Canada in 1949. Do you admit or do you deny that allegation?

A. I do not deny that allegation, but I will correct it by saying it was in 1948.

Q. Is it your testimony, then, that you admit that you last entered the United States at an unknown point across the boundary from Canada, but that you entered in 1948 rather than in 1949?

A. Yes, sir.

Q. Now, the fourth allegation, you failed to notify the Attorney General of your address during January 1956 and during January 1957. Do you admit or do you deny that allegation?

A. I admit it.

Q. Now, the fifth allegation, you did not furnish notice of your address because you feared that by so doing you would disclose *your illegal presence in the United States. Do you admit or do you deny that allegation?*

A. *I admit that, too.*

Q. *Now, the charge in the order to show cause and notice of hearing is that you are subject to deportation under Section 241(a)(5) of the Immigration and Naturalization Act and that you have failed to furnish notification of your address in compliance with the provisions of Section 265 and have not established that such failure was reasonably excusable or was not willful. Do you admit your deportability from the United States on this charge?*

A. *Yes.*

* * *

For almost six weeks—until August 7—Abel remained in custody at the immigration detention facility and was questioned daily by various FBI agents. They repeated the offer that if Abel would "cooperate," he would receive comfortable accommodations and even a government job with a US government agency in an attempt to turn Abel into a double agent. Abel refused to take the bait. During his sixth week, he was indicted on charges of conspiracy to commit espionage and ordered removed to New York City under authority of a bench warrant issued upon the indictment. The indictment charged him with the crime of espionage, a capital offense.

Abel then appeared in US district court in New York, and a plea of not guilty was entered. Abel was confined in the Federal Detention Headquarters at 427 West Street, where special precautions were taken to prevent him from committing suicide. According to an article in the *New York Herald Tribune*, dated August 12, 1957, "The Soviet Embassy in Washington, taking the traditional attitude of a government embarrassed by apprehension of an intelligence agent, has left the case to be treated as an internal concern of the United States."

James Donovan, Abel's court-appointed counsel, quickly determined that the only chance for his client was a violation of the search-and-seizure clause of the US Constitution. The Fourth Amendment provides: "The right of the people to be secure in their persons, houses, papers, and effects, against unreasonable searches and seizures, shall not be violated, and no Warrants shall issue; but upon probable cause, supported by Oath or affirmation, and particularly describing the place to be searched, and the persons or things to be seized."

On October 8th—less than a week before the trial was to begin—James Donovan promptly filed a motion to suppress the evidence that the INS officers had seized from Abel's room in the Hotel Latham. Donovan argued that the Constitution and laws of the United States are clear on the procedures which must be followed in arresting an individual and searching and seizing his property.

According to Donovan, the FBI—having reason to believe that a Russian spy was in Room 839 at the Hotel Latham—could have obtained a warrant for his arrest from a US commissioner or federal judge that charged him with espionage. The agents could have then searched the room and seized anything considered as instruments of committing espionage. Abel would then be promptly taken before the nearest available US commissioner or federal judge, where he would be entitled to consult counsel. Or, in the event FBI agents wished to search Room 839 without Abel present, they could have obtained a search warrant by complying with an equally clear and precise procedure.

Donovan explained that sometime before June 21, 1957, the Department of Justice, believing Abel to be a spy, had to make a decision. The FBI, Donovan noted, possesses the dual functions of a law enforcement agency and of a counterespionage arm of our national intelligence forces. The decision had to be made as to whether: (a) as law enforcement officers, they should arrest Abel on charges of espionage, conduct a lawful search and seizure, and follow all other procedures established under the Constitution and laws of the United States, or (b) as counterespionage agents fulfilling a national intelligence function, they should seize Abel, conceal his detention from his co-conspirators for the longest possible time, and seek to induce him to come over to our side.

Donovan wrote that, "The election between the two alternate courses of action was made. While that election may have been prospectively in the best interests of the United States, it did not succeed. The government thereafter cannot pretend that such an election was not made, or attempt to pay lip service to due process of law."

Donovan urged the court to conclude that the Fourth and Fifth Amendments to the Constitution had been violated. Donovan stated eloquently in his motion,

> "Abel is an alien charged with the capital offense of Soviet espionage. It may seem anomalous that our constitution guarantees protect such a man. The unthinking may view America's conscientious adherence to the principles of a free society as altruism so scrupulous that self-destruction must result. Yet our principles are engraved in the history and the law of this land. If the free world is not faithful to its own moral code, there remains no society for which others may hunger."

Donovan also argued in his motion to suppress the evidence seized at Abel's hotel room that a more practical and important consideration—turning Abel into a double agent—should have guided Abel's treatment:

> From June 21st to August 7th, Abel was treated by the Department of Justice, as a matter of law, as an alien illegally in the United States. Actually, however, it is evident that the department believed that he had committed the capital crime of

Russian espionage and this was the principal interest of the government in the man. Such undoubtedly was considered to be in our national interest.

Any person familiar with counter-espionage realizes that a defecting enemy agent can be of far greater value than one of our own operating agents. Not only is there the opportunity for our government to obtain complete information on the enemy's espionage apparatus but it can lead to such specifics as the names and locations of other enemy agents, the breaking of enemy ciphers, etc.

Moreover, there can be the possibility of using such a man as a "double agent" who, although believed by his original principals to be still working on their behalf, in reality is serving the other side.

Rudolf Abel told his counsel, James Donovan, that under no circumstance would he ever cooperate with the United States government or do anything to embarrass his country in order to save his own life. And, as it turned out, Abel would never stray from that position.

* * *

The vast number of items taken from Abel's hotel room and art studio would prove to be the most incriminating circumstantial evidence against him. Abel's room at the Hotel Latham was full of a multitude of items that make for interesting reading—rolls of film, small pieces of paper containing various cryptic handwritten notes, various keys, receipts, and pencils, to name a few:

- 3 metal containers of **35 mm film**
- 1 roll of Ektachrome **35 mm film**
- 1 strip of paper with four **typewritten lines** beginning with word "BALMORA" and ending with word "hand"
- 1 strip of paper with two **typewritten lines** beginning with word "Mr. VLADINEC" and ending with word "Jack"

- 1 strip of paper with **words**: "ALAN 100 HARV 100 BOX 20 RUT 100 TK 75"
- 1 slip of paper with **phrase** "As you told..." and ending with the word "ARRIVES"
- 1 strip of graph paper with **phrase** "In Mex." and ending with word "'BALMORA"
- 1 strip of paper containing two **typewritten lines** beginning with word "EMANUEL" and ending with word "GASTEIN"
- 1 green **aluminum container** and cap containing red lead pencil
- 1 red **notebook** whose first four pages contain handwritten notes
- 1 **key** stamped with the number "1077" and affixed to white tag with number "2508"
- 1 **key** stamped "L. L. BATES CO Boston"
- 1 **key** with metal identification tag noting number "2508" and green identification tag with notation "Safe Deposit Box"
- 1 Yale **key** stamped with serial number
- 1 key case containing six **keys**
- 1 strip of graph paper containing **series of digits** in groups of fives; first group of digits is identified as "02505" and last group is identified as "25658"
- 1 strip of graph paper containing six **lines** written in a foreign language
- 1 red-colored lead **pencil** identified as "ASTRA 1134T"
- 1 **metal lens** with rubber cap
- 1 **receipt** for sum of $200.85
- Camera Craft **receipt** for sum of $120.51

- 1 piece of graph paper with **figures** in upper left-hand corner
- 1 piece of graph paper with **word** "400 KC" on right-hand side
- 1 piece of graph paper with **word** "Lenses" in upper left-hand corner
- 1 piece of graph paper with **words** "Lathe 6 atlas" in upper left-hand corner
- 1 piece of graph paper with **number** "5a" in upper lefthand corner and "d-2" in lower right-hand corner
- 1 piece of graph paper with **words** "Oar with some tools" in upper left-hand corner
- 1 piece of graph paper with **formula** "n=nm+1 (M-1 etc.)"
- Sketchbook, whose first sheet has **words** "Good Luck and Happy Drawing"
- One International **Certificate of Vaccination** for Martin Collins
- 1 sheet memo paper with **words** "Victor—P-35.00" on it; 1 sheet of memo paper with total of "175.56" and "24,710" and one Bill #0014841 for $359.99
- 2 **coins**: one penny and one dime
- 2 **photographs**: one of a man and one of a woman, with names "Shirley" and "Morris" on back
- 1 piece of graph paper with the **notation** "SMTWTFS" in upper left-hand corner
- 1 piece of graph paper with **figure** 236.54 in upper right-hand corner
- 1 drawing **pen**
- 2 **matchbook** covers: "Daytona Plaza" and "Anthony's Italian Cuisine"
- 1 Hallicrafter Model S-38-D **radio**

* * *

Scattered about Abel's hotel room were also five leather cases. The first one contained primarily camera equipment, which was no doubt used for sending secret messages:

- 1 telescopic **lens** marked Ernst Leitz (#NR898785)
- 1 Leica **camera** and case
- 1 piece **chamois**
- 2 **lenses**
- 1 small **developing** container
- 1 **camera trigger** mechanism
- 1 Leica **meter** with leather case
- 1 pen **knife**
- 1 roll **film** in black plastic container
- 1 paper **tag** for "Japan Camera" dated June 1956
- 1 utility **knife**
- 1 telescopic **lens** labelled "E. Leitz-Wetzlar"
- 1 piece copper **wire**
- 1 **wallet**
- 1 **warranty** card from Canon Camera Co., 550 Fifth Ave., New York City
- 1 roll color **film** in white paper
- 1 small **lens**
- 15 **Band-aids**, 2 **buttons**, 1 **rubber band**, 1 white **handkerchief**
- 1 deck of **playing cards**
- 1 **container** marked "F:E;lRD, PIA.TNIK & SOHNE-Vienna"
- 2 boxes of "ready-mounts" for **transparencies**
- 11 **transparencies**—2 blank holders
- 1 package of **lens cleaning** paper

- 3 color **filters** in case
- 2 **lenses** & 8 cases
- 1 small black plastic-and-aluminum **container**
- 1 aluminum **cap**
- 1 brass **lens** in black case
- One **book** from Schneider & Co., 128 W. 58th, New York
- City-Artists **printed materials**
- One metal **container** containing artist's supplies and paintings and one New Year's card

* * *

A second brown leather briefcase contained various art supplies, probably used for Abel's passionate hobby of drawing:

- 1 package of **graph paper** sheets for ring binder
- 2 **record discs** by Julian Bream
- 1 **sketch pad** with drawings
- 7 **canvas paintings**, 6 blank canvases
- 1 pad of **graph paper**
- 1 **sketchbook**
- 1 green **pencil**
- 1 yellow **pencil**
- 1 **travel folder** for Silver Springs, Florida
- 12 air mail **envelopes** and writing paper

* * *

The third case—a brown leather suitcase—contained his decidedly drab wardrobe:

- 1 gray tweed **jacket** ("Wanamaker" label)
- 1 gray **jacket** ("John David" label)

- 3 pair gray **pants** ("DAKS" label)
- 1 oxford gray **pants** ("DAKS" label)
- 1 oxford gray **pants** ("Majer" label)
- 1 light gray **pants** ("DAKS" label)
- 1 light gray **pants** ("Majer" label)
- 8 **neckties** ("Dublin" label)
- 11 pairs of **socks**
- 2 pairs of **shorts**
- 3 **T-shirts**
- 1 sport **shirt**
- 1 pair checked **pajamas**
- 1 sleeveless **sweater**
- 33 **handkerchiefs**
- 3 **shirts**
- 1 **pajama top**
- 1 **sketch book**
- 2 painted **canvases**
- 1 index book for "Kodak" brand color **prints**
- 1 white porcelain **developing tray**
- 1 **statement** from Joseph Mayer Co. for $2.02

* * *

A fourth suitcase (marked with tag #452161) contained a range of miscellaneous items for daily living:

- 1 roll of toilet paper
- 1 eraser
- 1 metal pencil ("Conte a Paris" brand)
- 1 blue pencil—labelled "2B"—chisel point

- 1 green pencil—charcoal
- 1 broken metal yellow pencil
- 1 rain jacket and case
- 2 scarves
- 1 sweatshirt
- 1 roll of marking tape
- 1 black three-ring binder with paper
- 1 notebook pad of ("Block esquela" brand) 2d
- 1 "Peerless" white portable radio
- 1 transparency viewer
- 1 case toilet articles and pipe cleaners
- 13 greeting cards
- 1 Park Avenue portfolio with airmail envelopes and graph paper
- 1 self-portrait
- 2 dish towels
- 11 boxes drawing leads
- 1 book (*Art Treasures*)
- 1 business card for Ben (Hobo) Benson ("King of the Hoboes")
- 1 package foreign stamps
- 1 container "'Old Spice" shaving lotion
- 1 container "Old Spice" cologne
- 1 can foot powder
- 1 "Kimble" thermometer
- 2 pairs of reading glasses
- 6 packs of Winston cigarettes
- 1 alarm clock

- Assorted radio tubes
- 1 can athlete's foot powder
- 1 box paint color
- Assorted rolls green insulated wire
- 1 wiretap apparatus
- 1 pair pincers
- 1 film container
- 1 bottle aspirin
- 1 shaving brush
- 1 box containing screwdrivers
- 1 pair sunglasses
- 1 receipt for $29.40 from Hotel Latham dated 6/8/57
- Tobacco pouches (1 leather, 1 cellophane)
- Smoking pipes
- 2 pair socks
- 12 yellow pencils
- 1 box AMT antidepressant tablets
- 1 tube of "Lepages" glue
- 1 bottle athlete's foot lotion
- 1 container of "Stoppette" spray deodorant
- 1 ivory container
- 1 cigarette lighter
- Large erasers
- Oblong leads (drawing)
- 1 roll bandage
- 1 metal pipe cleaner
- 1 black rubber stopper
- 1 airmail stamp

- 2 books of matches
- 1 sheet for film processing—"Kodak" Processing Kit
- Miscellaneous paint brushes in black and white cloth
- 1 raincoat ("John David" label)
- 1 pair pants ("Casa Rionda" label)
- 1 pajama pants
- 4 handkerchiefs
- 1 blue shirt

* * *

And the last of the leather cases in the hotel room was a brown, zippered briefcase containing cash, various bills, and other items:

- 1 brown wallet with four fifteen-cent airmail stamps (containing pad with "SDBA 20" printed in upper left-hand)
- 10-cent stamps
- 2-cent stamps
- 1 card with words "Prince Gartner"
- 1 business card for "Harriet Lorence"
- 1 small package of notebook paper
- 1 green pencil ("Castell" brand)
- 1 red plastic mechanical pencil
- 1 circular piece of white metal similar to a pulley
- 1 checking register for East River Savings, showing balance of $1,386.22
- 3 receipts from Broadway Central (for Collins)
- 3 receipts from Daton Plazas (for Collins)
- 7 receipts from Hotel Latham (for Collins)
- 1 receipt from Fifth Avenue Laundry (for Collins)
- 1 receipt from Wright Arch Preserver (for Collins)

- 1 receipt from Peyton Ltd. (for Collins)
- 2 brown envelopes from Manufacturers Trust Co.
- Brown wallet in zipper briefcase containing cash: (1) 1 $20 bill with serial number D04553009 A (in one compartment of wallet), (2) 25 $20 bills, and (3) 10 $50 bills
- Brown paper wrapper in zippered briefcase containing cash: $4,000 in $20 bills.

The FBI inventory also noted that a birth certificate for Emil Robert Goldfus and a birth certificate for Martin Collins were found.

* * *

And yet, Abel's hotel room contained even more. Especially significant were items taken from the wastebasket, including microdot developer and a cipher pad for cryptography:

- Loose pieces of **paper** (one inch by two inch)
- 5 full and partially full boxes of f/2.8 9 oz. **microdot developer** ("Kodak" brand)
- 6 **books**: *The Penguin Hazel, Nights of Love and Laughter, The Ribald Reader, A Time to Love and a Time to Die, Three Plays*, and *Paintings from the San Paulo Museum*
- 1 partially used box of "Johnson & Johnson" **cotton balls**
- 1 can of "Aerolite" **wood adhesive**
- 1 partially full box of "Sheik" **prophylactics**
- 1 empty bottle of "Neo-synephrin" **nasal spray**
- 1 empty tin of "Sucrets" **cough drops**
- 1 box of "Ace" **bandages**, two-inch width
- 1 partially used tube of "Arex" **chap cream**
- 1 partially filled plastic bag of **tobacco**
- 1 empty **bottle**, unmarked, with "3iv" imprinted

- 1 partially used can of "Ronsonol" **lighter fluid**
- 1 piece **garnet paper** and rubbing block
- 1 roll of green, **coated wire**
- 4 **pencils** (three to five inches in length)
- 7 regular lead **pencils**
- 1 pair of white cotton **gloves**
- 1 white plastic **spray bottle**
- Two pieces of **coated wire** with green insulation

* * *

Perhaps most incriminating to Abel was the inventory of property taken from his art studio in Brooklyn, which contained, in addition to the usual innocuous items, a range of espionage tools—photographic equipment and small empty containers used for sending messages to the Soviet Union.

- 1 **book**: *The New Astronomy*
- 1 wooden **box** labeled "Swiss Files"
- 1 "Sucrets" brand cough drops box containing assorted **nails**
- 1 "Empire" brand clothes **brush**
- 1 "Wollensak Optical" brand **lens**
- 1 "Hallicrafter" grand **radio** (serial no. AB-475·506)
- 1 radio **speaker**
- 1 red box of 35mm color **slides**
- 1 "Sucrets" brand cough drops box filled with various small items, some of which were **hollow**, i.e., **cuff links** and **pieces of metal**
- 1 box marked "Jacobs Chucks" containing miscellaneous **radio parts** and two **cuff links**
- 1 "Norelco" brand shaving box containing **razor**, **cord**, two buttons, and one US 1902 **nickel**

- 1 "Sucrets" brand cough drops box containing **film strips**
- 1 "Sucrets" brand cough drops box containing miscellaneous **cuff links** and metal objects
- 1 red box containing miscellaneous **radio tubes**
- 1 **appointment card** for Dr. John J. Daub
- 1 "Martinson's Coffee" brand can sealed with adhesive tape, believed to contain **film**
- 1 cardboard box containing **tools, bolts,** and other miscellaneous items
- 1 small metal and wood **tool**
- 1 roll of 35mm **negatives** with "Berkeyn Photo Service" brand wrapper
- 1 red box marked "Pavelle" color containing **film strips**
- 1 "Hallicrafter" brand **radio** in brown leather carrying case
- 1 container "Kodak Ektachrome" brand safety **film**
- 1 wooden **box** containing three wooden **pencils,** a **bolt,** two **pieces of metal** with holes in each, a metal **gauge,** two **files,** miscellaneous pieces of **metal,** one **tack,** and one **clothes pin**
- 1 "Scholastic" brand **notebook**
- 1 **book:** *Cryptanalysis: A Study of Cyphers and Their Solutions*
- Metal containers of **film**
- 1 **map:** "Bear Mountain-Harriman Section, Palisades Interstate Park"
- Yellow cans of "Kodak" brand **film**
- 1 celluloid container, containing two **negatives,** and a handwritten note
- 1 paper-wrapped package of 35mm **slides**
- Envelope with what appears to be a **map** drawn on outside
- 35mm **slides**

- 1 box of "Kodak" brand sheet **film**
- 1 cardboard box containing unfinished **tubes**
- 1 **slide rule**
- 1 "Sucrets" brand cough drops **box** containing taps, rivets, washers, and a mirror wrapped in paper
- 1 **vacuum tube**
- Cardboard box containing envelopes of **photographic colors**
- Paper bag labeled "One quarter pound **gum tragacanth**"
- 1 **notebook**
- 1 box labelled "M & B Promicrol" with images of small **drills**, containing miscellaneous small tools.
- 1 **color slide** sealed around edges with paper
- 1 "RCA" **electron tube**
- 1 envelope of **pigment** marked "8 oz. Naples yellow lt."
- 1 "Bernz-0-Matic" brand propane torch **shaving brushes**
- 1 "Scotch" **tape** metal box
- 1 leather **strap** with two screws on catches
- 1 can of "Kodak Super XX" brand high-speed **film**, twenty exposures
- 1 can of "Kodak Plus X" brand safety **film**, thirty-six exposures
- 1 can of "Kodak Plus X" brand safety **film**, twenty exposures
- 1 "Standard Tool Company" envelope containing notations and **figures**
- 1 **invitation** from the president of the Council of National Academy of Design
- 1 white envelope containing **receipt** of sale, five rent receipts, and one woodland negative

- Plastic **cup** containing soft paper, waxes, and other miscellaneous items, including shaving brush
- 1 "Eicor" brand **tape recorder** with tape
- **Pencils**: #2 "Conte" and #2 "Eagle"
- 1 circular piece of **brass**
- "Audio Devices" brand spool-recorder **tape**
- 1 spool-recorder **tape** in unmarked white box
- 1 "Starrett" brand **micrometer** box and a small microscope kit in leather zipper case
- 1 **envelope** labelled "Sol Goldwasser, 191 Canal Street"
- **Photographs**
- 1 briefcase, leather, brown, containing many papers including **musical scores**
- Hollow **metal cylinders** with removal ends
- 1 Lincoln **penny** dated 1955
- 1 set of **drills** in "Great Lakes Steel Corporation" holder
- 1 red box marked "Leitz-Germany," containing two circular containers and five pieces of camera equipment **boxes**
- 24 small boxes, many of which contained **film**
- 1 "Weller" **soldering iron**
- 1 black paper **pad**
- 1 "Starrette" brand **micrometer** head
- 1 metal **flashlight** containing two batteries
- 1 wooden **box** containing watchmaker's screw plate and tools
- 1 torn paper **bag** containing nuts, washers, bolts, and eight screws on bottle caps
- 1 "Harrison" **color attachment**
- 1 small metal **punch**

- 1 camera **lens**
- 1 brass **gauge**
- 1 watchmaker's **eyepiece**
- 1 small piece of wood containing four **dots**
- 1 box containing "Adapt-A-Roll 620" brand **camera equipment**
- 1 case containing "Nomis Company" **compass set**
- 1 small "Huot" drill index with **drills**
- 1 piece of white paper with the **words** "510 E ll HLWild"
- 1 box "JY-horse" hand **taps**
- 1 "Lufkin" brand screw **pitch gauge**
- **Thermometers**
- 1 "Hagstrom" brand **map** of Queens, New York
- 1 metal **pencil** in plastic box containing film, "Kodak" **photographic reducer, stain remover**
- 1 "Dormeyer" brand #200 **drill**
- 1 **magnifying glass**
- 1 **thank you note** from Mr. & Mrs. Burton Silverman
- 1 **business card** for White-Hixon Laboratories Inc.
- 1 roll of "Kodak Super XX" brand **film**, thirty-six exposures
- 1 roll of "Kodak Ektachrome" brand **film**
- 1 Phillips-type **screwdriver** marked "Stanley #2732"
- 1 black **fountain pen**
- 1 "Hensoldt Wetzlar" brand **magnifying glass**
- Green crayon **pencils**
- 1 envelope containing **drawing paper**, graph paper, and various technical pamphlets
- 1 color **slide** of woods scene
- 1 paper bag containing **chalk**

- 1 "Premier" brand street **map** of Chicago
- 1 "Hagstroms" brand **map** of Brooklyn
- 1 "Texaco" brand New York street **map**
- 35mm strips of **film**
- 1 gray **scratch pad**
- **Receipts** from Lincoln Warehouse, New York City
- 1 box of **filter paper**
- 1 "Sinclair" brand **map** of New York and metropolitan New York
- 1 "Texaco" brand **map** of New York and Long Island
- 1 **passbook** for National City Bank of New York, 96 St. Branch
- **Sketchbooks**
- **Matchbooks**
- **Assorted pencils**
- 6 **screws**
- Boxes of photographic paper containing **photographs**
- 1 **speaker** mounted on cardboard
- 1 **record player**
- 1 clip pad with mathematical **formulas**
- 1 gray **note pad** with notation "UN 5-4000"
- 1 box containing 35mm **film**, tacks, and matches
- 1 round plastic case containing some type of **thread**
- Gray, cardboard, **pencil-shaped objects**
- 1 yellow envelope containing small **pieces of metal**
- **Photographs** of men and one of girl
- 1 "Hoffritz Cutlery" **receipt**
- 1 international **mail schedule**

- 1 "Nikkor" lenses **pamphlet**
- 1 **book**: *Van Gogh*
- 1 "Sucrets" brand cough drops box containing miscellaneous **tacks**
- Numerous musical score **books** and technical pamphlets
- 1 wooden **box** containing "Jap—Art Kolor Stix"
- 1 piece of cardboard containing three blue **thumbtacks**
- "Sucrets" brand cough drops boxes containing miscellaneous **screws and washers**
- 1 small piece of **metal pipe**
- 1 paperbound **book**: *Murder on the Side*
- 1 **photograph** of man with stick
- 1 yellow "Anco" brand clasp envelope with numerous **papers** inside
- 1 balance to thirty-five-inch **weights**
- 1 **guitar pick** and case
- 1 **map** of Chicago "Loop"
- 1 package of twenty-two phonograph **records**
- Miscellaneous small **tools**
- 1 coil of gray **wire**
- 1 coil of blue **wire**
- 1 bundle of three phonograph **records**
- 1 paperbound **book**: *The Last Party*
- 1 oil **painting** of refinery
- 1 small piece of **wood** glued together
- **Matchboxes**
- 1 red **plastic object**
- Various **notebooks**, photographs, art sketchbooks, scientific magazines

- 1 picture **postcard** to "Goldfus from Gladys"
- Pieces of **wood**, showing signs of having been glued together
- 1 piece of **wood** showing attempts to alter outer edge
- 1 piece of **foam rubber** glued together
- 1 "Eveready" brand flashlight **battery**
- 1 "Bright Star" brand flashlight **battery**
- 64 artist's **paint brushes** and three pencils
- 1 plastic **container** with blue top
- 1 light metal **container**, threaded inside with hole in bottom
- 1 "Orie Speedgraphic" **camera**, serial number #E88035
- 1 bottle **diethylene oxide** from Amend Drug & Chemio
- Magna-grips **rivets**
- 1 "Schneider-Krueznach" brand **lens**
- 1 "Gorez double anastigmatic" **lens**
- **Photograph** of market which is overlined and one overliner
- 1 "Premier" brand street **map** of Baltimore
- 1 "Sinclair" brand **map** of Long Island
- 1 "Sinclair" brand **map** of Westchester and Putnam Counties
- 13 sales and rent **receipts**
- **News clipping** containing death notices on one side and notice of arrest on other
- 1 group of **photographic paper**
- 1 **book**: *Elements of Symbolic Logic*
- 1 **book**: *World Famous Paintings*
- 1 **bookmark** from "Concord Books"
- 1 **book**: *Science News*
- **Miscellaneous items,** photographic equipment, pencils, electronic tubes, matchbooks, map covers, French dictionary

- 1 book: *The Artist's Handbook*
- 1 book: *Number: The Language of Science*
- 1 book: *Installation and Operations Instructions for Model S-72 Portable Radio Receiver*
- 1 book: *Degas*
- 1 book: *Silver for the Craftsman*
- 1 book: *Hands*
- 1 book: *Vuillard*
- 1 book: *Kaethe-Kollwitz*
- 1 book: *The Journey of Simon McKeever*
- 1 book: *The Continental*
- 1 book: *Goya to Gauguin*
- 16 photographs
- 1 hollowed-out large nail
- 1 set of headphones
- Miscellaneous items found on second shelf: matchbook, photographic equipment, checkbook
- 1 piece of two-by-four wood studs glued together
- 10 tacks and miscellaneous electrical equipment
- 1 "Seth Thomas" metronome
- 1 envelope containing sandpaper
- 1 envelope containing small pieces of plywood glued together
- Miscellaneous items found on bottom shelf of closet: maps, photographs, portraits, photography equipment, brochures, and books
- Miscellaneous papers containing notes and photographs

* * *

And then there were the contents of the storage unit near the art studio—which was the most incriminating espionage evidence of all:

- 1 "Eico" **signal generator**, #A-2877
- 1 box of "Kodak" **sheet film**
- 1 **wire** with two clamps
- 1 "Kodak" **densitometer** model lA
- 1 "Greenfield" **screw plate**, #A-1½
- 1 round metal box containing **screws**
- "Kodak" sheet film box, containing **screws** and **gears**
- "Kodak" sheet film box, containing **screws** and **negatives**
- Red cardboard box containing **screws**
- 1 **lamp**
- 1 black metal box appearing to be **photocell**
- 1 "Kine Exakta" **multiscope**, with six canisters of film
- 2 **keys**
- 1 "Ronson" **cigarette lighter**
- 1 box "Dupont Defender" **film**
- 3 **keys** on ring
- 1 hand-type **film editor** with 35 mm film attached
- 1 "Etalom" T-square-type **wrench** in case
- 1 **book** entitled *Schwann*
- 2 wooden **pencils**
- 1 hard rubber tank containing various **metal objects**
- 1 box (wooden), three inches by seven inches, containing miscellaneous items including three **tie clasps**
- 1 small hand **blowtorch**
- 1 box of "Kodachrome" **film**
- 1 box of "Kodachrome" **film**, unsealed

- 1 glass cutter
- 1 metal turning **lathe** and accessories in wooden box
- 1 city **map** and tourist guide of Los Angeles
- 1 package of **plastic pieces**
- 6 metallic **film canisters** (sealed)
- 1 "Canon" **camera holder** in leather case
- 1 metal **film canister**
- 1 "Sucrets" box containing **nuts and bolts**
- 2 metallic **film canisters** (sealed)
- 1 set of "Elson" **taps and dies**
- 1 box, three and one-fourth inches by four and one-fourth inches, entitled **screws, bolts,** etc. to easel
- 1 cardboard box one-and-a-half feet by two feet by one-half foot, containing **books**
- 1 cardboard box containing a **lathe** and miscellaneous **machine parts**
- 1 roll **gummed paper** from William I. Meil, 1507 Walnut St., Philadelphia
- 1 "Sucrets" box containing various **screws** and **metal objects**
- 1 "Jacobs" chucks box containing various **metal objects**
- 1 black loose-leaf **notebook**
- 1 box, eight by ten inches, containing various **lenses and prisms**
- 1 notebook, eight by ten inches, containing **receipts and numerous notes**
- 1 container "Ansco" color 35mm **film**
- 1 long **screw** about five inches
- 1 canister with several strips 35mm **film**
- 1 "Sucrets" box containing **screws**

- 1 "Western Incident" **light adapter** consisting of two parts
- 1 "Sucrets" box containing **screws**
- 1 Zippo-type **lighter**
- 1 cardboard box with red plastic tape containing **screws**
- 1 "Leica" 35mm **printer**
- 1 **solder** and flux kit
- 1 "Bietgen" 1931 B-8 **protractor**
- 1 solid metallic **circular object** of same size
- 1 plastic box containing **screws** and **metal objects**
- 1 cardboard box marked separation negatives, containing various **metal objects**
- 1 set "Henry & Allen" **tin shears**
- 1 cardboard box, four by one by one-and-a-half inches, containing **screws** and other **metal objects**
- 4 ounces (two sheets) imported rabbit skin **glue**
- 1 red colored **pencil**
- 2 packages "Kodak Ektachrome" color **film**
- 1 plastic bottle containing **gears** in oil
- 1 box containing **mirror**, one-and-a-half by one-and-a-half inches
- 1 plastic box, two by two inches, containing numerous small, watch-type parts
- 1 small coil of green **wire**
- 1 "Simpson" **meter**
- 1 "Westinghouse" **voltmeter**
- 1 package metal **film mounts**
- 1 **book** entitled *History* by V. Gordon Childe
- 2 large glass **magnifiers**
- 1 bottle Phenylenediamine **chemicals**

- 1 bottle Acetoacet-yellow **chemicals**
- Small paper bag containing **toggle switch** and other **metal objects**
- 1 ANW 250 **instrument**
- 1 piece plain white **paper** with writing
- 4 **tools**, one ten-inch screwdriver, one twelve-inch file, one ten-inch square, one six-inch file
- 1 "Electro-Tech" **meter**
- 1 piece of graph paper with **writing**
- 1 large **magnifying glass**
- 1 box containing two **pencils** and miscellaneous items
- Miscellaneous **papers** found in rubber band—two maps, photo, and graph paper
- 1 box of **radio parts** and tubes
- 1 twelve-inch flexible **curve rule**
- 1 box containing miscellaneous items—pen, pencil, nails, screws, **film**, and **radio parts**
- 1 cardboard box containing **radio tubes**
- 1 cardboard box containing one-third horsepower "Atlas" **motor** and various items
- 1 metal container containing **radio parts** and screws
- 2 metal-bound **magnifying glasses**
- 1 box containing **radio parts, film containers, matches, screws, pencils**
- 1 "Assembly Products Inc." **meter**
- 1 box of miniature **electronic tubes**
- 1 box containing "Arista" **grid light enlarging unit**
- 1 box of radio tubes and **flash lamps**
- 4 miscellaneous **radio tubes** and two **electronic circuits**

- 1 cardboard box marked "Bending Jigs" containing **metal objects**
- 1 box of **radio parts**
- 1 box of glass jars containing **photographic chemicals**
- 1 "Sucrets" box containing **screws**
- 1 **book**: *How to Run a Lathe*
- 1 box containing jars of **chemicals**
- 2 jars of citric acid **chemicals**
- 1 jar potassium metabisulfite **chemicals**
- 1 box containing a **motor** and **lathe parts**
- 1 package strip **film**
- 1 "Aristo" brand **enlarging unit** for color model 5x7
- 1 jar acid pyrogallic **chemicals**
- 1 photo **enlarger**
- 1 "Hagstrom" **map** of New Jersey
- 1 "Hagstrom" **map** of fifty-mile radius from New York
- 1 "Hagstrom" **map** of New York City
- 1 small black **transformer**
- 1 typewritten set of **notes** entitled "That You Cannot Mix Art And Politics"
- 1 large **slide rule**
- 1 camera case containing **camera** Ser. #M-69121
- 1 **photo enlarger**
- 1 box marked "**Small motors, volt stabilizers and heavy electronics**"
- 1 "Gralab" **timer**
- 1 **transformer**
- 1 box of "Eagle" color **pencils**
- 1 three-inch metal **pipe**

- 1 "Diacro" twelve-inch **shears** enclosed in wooden case
- 1 "Diacro" twelve-inch **brake**
- 1 black **application for social security account number**, found in suitcase (blue with brown trim)
- One **key**

CHAPTER NINE

A bel's trial began as the bailiff entered the New York City courtroom and sharply announced to the lawyers, jury members, and spectators gathered there: "All rise. The federal district court for the eastern district of the state of New York calls to order case number 45094, United States of America versus Rudolf Ivanovich Abel, also known as 'Mark,' and also known as Martin Collins and Emil R. Goldfus, with the Honorable Judge Mortimer W. Byers presiding."

Judge Byers, who was eighty-one years old, had served as a federal judge for twenty-eight years and had presided over Nazi spy trials in 1941. He was known as a stern judge with strong convictions. The judge nodded to the prosecution to begin.

William F. Tompkins, a slender forty-four-year-old who had been a military prosecutor and a prolific prosecutor in the Justice Department's Internal Security division, would argue the case for the government, along with assistant attorneys Kevin J. Maroney, James J. Featherstone, and Anthony R. Palermo. Tompkins walked toward the jury.

"May it please the court, ladies and gentlemen of the jury:

"It is our duty to present the evidence that has been assembled by the investigative agencies of the government and to prove the truth of the charges set forth by the grand jury. My colleagues and myself are conscious of our obligation to represent the government of the United States and the people of the United States, and conscious of the obligation to protect the rights of the individual defendant as well as the rights of all American citizens by proceeding diligently against those who have transgressed our law and who, perhaps, have dedicated themselves to the destruction of our country.

"I want to make this very clear. The interest of the government is not that we shall win a case, but that justice shall be done. In other words, that innocence shall not suffer, nor guilt escape. In accordance with that, I want to pledge to you on behalf of my colleagues and myself that we will conduct ourselves in such a fashion that this defendant will be insured a fair trial.

"The nature of the charge is one of unusual significance, and it takes on added significance when you consider that it occurred during critical years of our history. However, the seriousness of the charge does not make it a difficult one. The grand jury indictment is simple, and I just want to talk to you about that for a few minutes. I first of all say this: The indictment is a charge; it is not proof of anything."

Tompkins then summarized the indictment, beginning with the fist count, in which the grand jury charged the defendant with "conspiracy to commit espionage and with conspiring with other conspirators to transmit information relating to our national defense." Tompkins listed the defendant's spying devices and techniques—the short-wave radio, the hollowed-out containers, the "drops" in the city parks, large sums of money, forged birth certificates, and fake passports. And he mentioned, "And it was also charged by the grand jury that in the event of war between the United States and Russia, the conspirators would set up clandestine radio transmitters and receiving posts for the purpose of continuing to furnish information to Russia."

Referring to the overt acts listed in support of the indictment, Tompkins said, "I am going to talk very generally about these, because I feel it is far more preferable that you hear the testimony from the mouths of witnesses rather than lawyers."

"As you know, you are the sole judges of the truth and the facts, and the court is the sole judge of the law. The evidence and the corroboration will come from various witnesses. It will be direct evidence. The government will present circumstantial evidence, and one of the witnesses will be a member of this conspiracy—a co-conspirator who was selected by the other conspirators to participate.

"Invariable experience, I may as well say to you, shows that the defense will attack him. However, I think you should remember this: The co-conspirator has now left the conspiracy. He is no longer adding to his past sins, and he is telling the truth. His testimony will be corroborated, and by corroboration I mean confirmation—confirmation by the testimony of other witnesses and by documentary evidence and by admissions of the defendant. It is evidence which the government feels cannot be contradicted because it is the truth, and it will prove beyond any doubt the guilt of the defendant.

"We shall prove that the defendant—a colonel in the Soviet State Security Service—together with other high-ranking Russian officials, put into operation a most elaborate apparatus of Soviet intelligence and espionage in an endeavor to secure our most important secrets—secrets of great importance to this country as well as the free world."

Tompkins then discussed Abel's history in the United States since 1948, and that he was later joined by an assistant in 1952. But in May 1957, Tompkins maintained, the conspiracy collapsed.

"One of the co-conspirators defected, and he related his story to American officials abroad. The FBI, in their very vigilant and efficient manner, conducted an investigation—a very intensive investigation—which resulted in the uncovering of overwhelming and devastating corroboration of the defendant's guilt.

"Now, in conclusion, let me say this to you: The government feels that the evidence we will adduce before this jury will prove to you not only beyond a reasonable doubt, but beyond any possible doubt, the guilt of the defendant. In other words, the evidence will clearly point to one and only one possible verdict—that of guilty as charged by the grand jury."

* * *

Defense attorney Donovan then presented his opening.

"May it please the court, ladies and gentlemen of the jury:

"This is a case which you, the jury, after hearing the evidence presented and under instructions of the judge, are to decide whether or not the defendant has been proven guilty beyond a reasonable doubt of a crime for which he could be sentenced to death.

"The prosecutor has outlined for you the nature of the charges and has described the evidence which he contends will prove these charges. It is important to remember, with respect to the three counts in this indictment, that it is only under count number one, that is, the conspiracy to transmit information to Russia, that the defendant could be sentenced to death.

"Now, I am the attorney for the defendant. I was assigned this task by the court, and under our system of American justice it will be my duty throughout this proceeding to represent the interests of the defendant in every respect. This is done, under our law, so that you may know the truth and render a just verdict.

"This case is not only extraordinary, it is unique. For the first time in American history, a man is being threatened with death as a sentence on the charge that he acted as a spy for a foreign nation with which we are legally at peace.

"The defendant is a man named Abel. It is most important that you keep that fact uppermost in your mind throughout the days ahead. This is not a case against communism. It is not a case against Soviet Russia. Our grievances against Russia have been voiced and are being voiced every day in the United Nations and in various other forums. But the sole issues in this case, on which you are going to render the verdict, deal with whether or not this man Abel has been proved guilty beyond a reasonable doubt of the specific crimes with which he is now charged.

"The prosecution has just told you that among the principal witnesses against the defendant will be a man—whose name is Häyhänen—who claims that he helped the defendant to spy against the United States.

"This means that within a very short while, this man will take the stand and testify before you. Observe his demeanor very carefully. Bear in mind that if what the government says is true, it means that this man has been here for some years living among us, spying on behalf of Soviet Russia. In order to do this it means, and it is so charged in the indictment, that he entered the United States on false papers, that he swore falsely in order to obtain these papers, that he has lived here every day only by lying about his true identity, about his background, about every facet of his everyday life.

"Furthermore, if what the government says is true, he was being paid to do this by Soviet Russia, and we can assume that if Russia properly trains her spies, he was trained abroad in what his 'cover' should be here, meaning that he was trained in the art of deception. He was trained to lie. In short, assuming that what the government says is true, this man is literally a professional liar.

"Now, bear this in mind as you hear his testimony. Bear also in mind that if what the government has told you is true, it means that this man has committed many crimes against our laws, including the capital offense of conspiring to transmit information to Russia. He has not yet been indicted for any of these crimes, and bear in mind that the man's sole hope of clemency, presumably, is not only that he implicate as many as he can in his crimes, but that he make as important as possible the information which he says he has to give to our government.

"Simply bear these facts in mind when you consider what motivation the witness has to tell the truth. And what justification or motivation he would have to do again what he has been doing for some years, and that is lying. Observe the demeanor of all these witnesses carefully.

"Remember at all times that the only evidence that can be presented in this case—the only evidence which you can consider—must come from the witness stand. The indictment is not evidence. What the prosecution counsel may say or I may say is not evidence. Remember at all times that a man's life can depend on your conscientious performance of your duty.

"Throughout this trial you will hear the judge and us lawyers refer to the prosecution as 'the government.' Now, that is precisely correct. But remember that in a larger sense, His Honor the judge, all counsel, and especially you represent the government of the United States. We all have precisely the same aim—a just verdict under the law.

"I know this jury will do its conscientious duty and render a just verdict in the tradition of a fair American trial."

* * *

Other than a truckload of espionage equipment seized from Abel's hotel room and art studio, the government had little to present other than the incriminating testimony of Reino Häyhänen, who was called to the stand. Donovan described Häyhänen's testimony as a "halting but fascinating recital of his complicated life as a Soviet espionage agent in New York City" and "an admixture of the bizarre, the startling, and sometimes the ludicrous as he told of drops, signal areas, visual meetings, soft film, magnetic containers, and secret messages in hollowed-out flashlight batteries."

After the prosecutor established Häyhänen's early years, he turned to Häyhänen's activities after he had secured his US passport and was returning to Moscow for additional training before he relocated to the states.

"Now, did you return to Moscow?" asked the prosecutor.

"Yes, I was called to Moscow in August, 1952."

"How did you return to Moscow?"

"I returned to Moscow by the train from Porkkala territory to Leningrad and from Leningrad to Moscow."

"How did you cross the border?"

"I crossed the border the same way like I came from Finland, in the trunk of the car," said Häyhänen.

"When you arrived in Moscow, what did you do?"

"When I arrived to Moscow, I met my bosses and I got new instructions, written instructions, what I have to do in the United States."

"Now, how long were you in Moscow on this trip?" the prosecutor asked.

"I cannot remember exact date when I came to Moscow, but it was second part of August and I left the third of September, 1952. About three weeks."

"Now, did you receive any training on this trip?"

"Yes, I got more training in photography, especially in making microdots, then in making soft film, then I got code—how to cipher and decipher some secret messages."

"Did you receive a code name while you were there?"

"Yes, because I am leaving Finland and the United States, I have to use a code name 'Vic.'" replied Häyhänen.

"Now, while you were in Moscow, did you see any containers?"

"Yes, I saw some containers, and I got training how to hide some messages in those containers and how to use those containers."

"Will you describe the containers just roughly? What kind of containers were they?"

Häyhänen explained in his broken English, "The containers, they are that kind of some hollow thing where you can hide some soft film or usual film. Suppose coin you can open it a special way and to put message over there and to close it. Or some bolts, screws, matchbooks, or some magazines."

"Now, on this trip to Moscow, did you meet Pavlov? Will you tell us first of all who he is?"

"Pavlov was in 1952 assistant boss to American section of espionage work."

"Did you see in Moscow, that trip, Mikhail Svirin?"

"Yes, I did," said Häyhänen.

"Would you tell us about him?"

"They explained to me that Svirin came for vacation to Moscow, and he is assigned to Soviet official work in the United States, and I have to meet him and have contact with him when I will come to New York."

"Did you have any conversation with him?"

"Yes," said Häyhänen, "I had just a short conversation and he was talking in general about New York City and about life in New York City, that the best part New York City was I have to find some apartment or furnished room when I will come to New York."

"Did Svirin tell you what his job was?"

"No, I didn't know his job, but I knew that he was in official work."

"Did you know whether he was attached to the UN delegation?"

"No, I didn't know it."

The prosecutor then asked, "At the time you were in Moscow in 1952, were you given any written or oral instructions?"

"I got written instructions, and I got oral instructions, too."

"Would you tell us from whom you got these written instructions?"

"Pavlov," said Häyhänen.

"Now, when Pavlov handed you those instructions, what did you do?"

"I read those instructions twice and I had to sign them."

"Do you remember the contents of those written instructions generally?"

Häyhänen replied, "Generally, there was that I will be sent to New York City as 'Mark's' assistant."

"At that time, did you know the name of the resident agent?"

"No, at that time I didn't know the name, but they told in New York there is some illegal espionage officer and, as they call it in Russian, resident, and that I will be sent as his assistant."

"Would you tell us what those instructions contained?"

Häyhänen replied, "Those instructions contained that as 'Mark's' resident assistant, I will get some espionage information from those illegal agents."

"Now, where were you to get these illegal agents, did the instructions say?"

"Yes, those instructions said that those illegal agents I will get from Soviet official people."

"By Soviet official people, what do you mean?" asked the prosecutor.

"I mean Soviet officials who are coming to the United States or to some other country by Soviet passports."

"Did your instructions contain anything relative to money?"

Häyhänen responded, "In the same instructions, there was that I will get $5,000 money for cover work, and that I will get salary $400 a month plus $100 for trip expenses. That will be salary what I am getting in the United States and then another salary what I was getting in Russian currency. It was different but I left to my relatives."

"Now, at the time that you received these written instructions from Pavlov, did you have a conversation with him?"

"Yes, I did."

"Did you receive oral instructions from him?"

"Yes, I did."

"Will you tell us about that, please?" asked the prosecutor.

"Pavlov explained me that on espionage work we are all the time in war, that I don't have to move to forget about espionage work. Even if they won't have any connections with me, so still I have to do my espionage work in the country where I was assigned.

And he explained that after war our country will ask from everyone what he did to win this war."

"During this conversation, or during the receipt of these oral instructions from Pavlov, did he give you any directions as to the type of information?"

"Yes, he did," said Häyhänen, "He told that it depends what kind of illegal agents I will have. It depends then what kind of information they can give, where they work, or whom they have as friends, and such and such things. He told that I have to consider with their help in every different occasion with every different agent."

"Now, let me ask you this directly—what type of information were you seeking?"

"Espionage information," Häyhänen replied.

The prosecutor asked for further clarification. "Would you describe that—what you mean by 'espionage information'?"

"By espionage information, I mean all information what you can look to get from newspapers or official way, by asking from, I suppose, legally from some office. And I mean by espionage information that kind of information what you have to get illegal way. That is, it is secret information concerning national security."

"What do you mean by 'national security?'"

"I mean some military information or atomic secrets."

"Now, as I understand, your testimony was that your instructions were to get secret information, is that correct?"

"That's right."

"Those were the oral instructions you were given by Pavlov?"

"Yes," said Häyhänen.

"By secret information, as I understand it, you mean atomic energy or defense information, isn't that correct?"

"That's right."

* * *

The prosecutor next elicited testimony from Häyhänen concerning a description of his activities after he moved to the United States.

"Mr. Häyhänen, when did you first enter the United States?"

"In October, 1952."

"And did you have a passport?"

"Yes, I did."

"What was the name on that passport?" asked the prosecutor.

"Eugene Nicoli Maki."

"Did you enter the United States in 1952 in connection with your employment by the government of the USSR?"

Häyhänen replied, "That is right, I did."

The prosecutor asked, "What were your duties on behalf of the Russian government in this country?"

"I was sent to this country to be resident assistant in espionage work."

"Now, do you know the name of the resident officer?"

"I know him just by the nickname 'Mark,'" said Häyhänen.

"Do you know him by any other name?"

"No, I don't. I didn't know him by other name. I know him just for security reasons by his nickname."

"Now, do you see him in the courtroom here?"

"Yes, I do," replied Häyhänen.

"Would you please point him out?"

"Yes, he is sitting there at the end of that table [indicating]."

The prosecutor then directed his attention to Rudolf Abel, "Will the defendant stand up, please?"

And Abel slowly stood up.

"Is that the gentleman?" asked the prosecutor.

"Yes."

Abel sat back down.

The prosecutor asked, "Now, do you know what his occupation is?"

"He told me that he worked as a photographer, that he had somewhere a photo studio."

"Do you know whether he is an employee of the USSR?"

"Yes, he was, or he was up to this time," said Häyhänen.

"And what agency of the government, if you know, was he employed by?"

"Yes, he was employed by KGB."

"Did he have any rank?"

Häyhänen replied, "Yes, he had the rank of colonel."

"Now, when did you first meet 'Mark'?"

"I met him in 1954, the first time."

"Did you see him subsequently?"

"Yes, then I was meeting him mostly once or twice a week," responded Häyhänen.

"When did you last see him before today?"

"The last I saw this year, February, middle of February, 1957."

* * *

The prosecutor completed his questioning of Häyhänen, and then it was time for Donovan to conduct his cross-examination of the prosecution's most important witness. Donovan had but one objective: to discredit Häyhänen by showing that he was a lazy, alcoholic bigamist who consistently beat his current wife.

Donovan started with Häyhänen's bigamy issue.

"Mr. Häyhänen, I show you Defendant's Exhibit D for identification, and which purports to be an original agreement signed between Tri-Berg, Incorporated, as landlord, and Eugene Maki and Hanna Maki. I ask you whether or not you recognize this agreement?"

"Yes, I do," replied Häyhänen.

"And did you sign that agreement?"

"Yes, I did."

"And did your wife sign it?"

"Yes, she did."

"I believe, Mr. Häyhänen, that you have testified that in February, 1953, your wife joined you in the United States, is that correct?"

"That is right."

"And I believe that you have testified that you were married in 1951?" asked Donovan.

"That is right."

"Isn't it a fact, Mr. Häyhänen, that at the time you say that you married in 1951, you already had a wife and child?"

"It is," replied Häyhänen.

"So as I understand your testimony, you are testifying that you have been a bigamist?" asked Donovan.

The prosecutor objected, "Now, if your Honor please, I think his testimony speaks for itself."

The judge agreed, "I don't think he needs to characterize the legal effect of his testimony."

Donovan proceeded with a new question, "Is it legal in Russia to have two wives at once?"

The prosecutor objected once again, and the court sustained the objection.

Donovan resumed his questioning of Häyhänen.

"And referring, Mr. Häyhänen, to Defendant's Exhibit C, consisting of these certified copies of passport documents, is it not a fact that in this passport application upon which your passport was issued December 4, 1956, and signed by you, that in response to the question 'present full legal name of spouse,' you wrote 'Hanna Maki' and stated as to the date of your marriage that you were last married on November 25, 1951?"

"That is right," replied Häyhänen.

"And yet you admit that on November 25, 1951, you had a wife and son in Russia, is that right?" asked Donovan.

"It was part of my legend because—that is why I wrote—answered this way questions," replied Häyhänen.

Donovan persisted. "I asked you a simple question. On November· 25, 1951, is it not a fact you had a wife and son in Russia?"

"It is," admitted Häyhänen.

"To the best of your knowledge, do you still have a wife and son in Russia?"

"I don't know," said Häyhänen.

"Who joined you in February, 1953?" asked Donovan.

"My wife by church marriage."

"What is her name?"

"Hanna Maki," replied Häyhänen.

"And is this the Mrs. Maki who signed the lease with you on the Bergen Street premises?"

"Yes, she is."

* * *

Donovan continued with his interrogation of Häyhänen, but this time it concerned his laziness and his spousal abuse.

"Now your testimony, as I understand it, Mr. Häyhänen, is that you leased these premises in Bergen Street to serve as a cover for espionage work. Is that correct?"

"It is," said Häyhänen.

"You say you leased these premises to set up an espionage cover under the guise of a photography shop, is that correct?"

"It is."

"Did you ever open up any such shop?" asked Donovan.

"No," replied Häyhänen.

"Is it a fact you boarded up the front window so as to completely close out any light?"

"I didn't board it."

"What did you do with respect to the front windows?"

Häyhänen replied, "I put glass wax on front windows because they have been dirty, and I left that glass wax on those windows up to opening of that business. And because I didn't open, I didn't wash those—that glass wax off."

"Could the ordinary person see from the outside through the glass wax?"

"Yes, because it was not so thick, and many people been looking through that glass wax."

"How long were you there?" Donovan asked.

"About one year," replied Häyhänen.

"During that time, when you had this espionage cover, you had this photographic shop that never opened and that had glass wax covering the front windows, is that right?"

"That's right."

Donovan then asked, "Now, I want you to think very carefully, Mr. Häyhänen. While you were living at that address with wife number two—"

The prosecutor interrupted with an objection, "Oh, now, if your Honor please, I don't think that is fair to characterize—"

The judge, somewhat whimsically, ruled, "I suppose that numerically he is correct, isn't he?"

Donovan resumed the questioning. "Now, I want you to think very carefully, search your recollection on this. While you were living there, was an ambulance ever called to attend you?"

"Yes."

"Did the police call that ambulance?"

"No."

"Would you kindly explain how the ambulance was called?" Donovan asked.

Häyhänen replied, "Landlord came to see us, and he called an ambulance."

"If you know, what was the reason why the ambulance arrived?"

"We been packing everything what was ours to move out from that storage, and when I was cutting rope from one package my hand with knife just went around and I cut my leg."

"How severe was this wound?" Donovan asked.

"It was maybe one-and-a-half inch," said Häyhänen.

"Isn't it a fact that the reason the landlord called the ambulance was that blood was all over the premises?"

"Yes. Not all over, but in couple rooms."

Donovan went further. "Yes, and isn't it a fact that, I ask you, wife number two had stabbed you in a drunken brawl? Isn't that true?"

"No, it is not. I can answer more if you like about that whole situation."

"If you deny that she stabbed you, there is not anything more I can do at this time."

Häyhänen protested, "She did not. She did not."

"Isn't it true," Donovan asked, "that the police on various occasions visited your premises?"

"On various occasions, no," denied Häyhänen.

"On several?" Donovan questioned.

"Just only one."

"Would you explain the circumstances?"

"Like I explained already, that when they called an ambulance, with ambulance came some police," said Häyhänen.

"I am not referring to that occasion," said Donovan, "I am asking you whether or not the Newark police came to your premises at any other time, to your knowledge, while you were living there?"

"They never been in our premises when we been living over there," insisted Häyhänen.

Donovan wouldn't let up. "Isn't it true that you had been beating your wife?"

"No, it is not," protested Häyhänen.

Donovan changed the subject. "Do you remember the bakery store next to 806 Bergen Street?"

"Yes, I remember," said Häyhänen.

"Is it not true that one day you entered that store with your wife, bought a loaf of bread, and threw it on the floor and ordered the woman to pick it up? Is that true or false?"

Häyhänen dodged the question. "I cannot recall that kind of thing right now."

Donovan was not about to relent. "You mean this is an ordinary incident and you just wouldn't recall it?"

"No," said Häyhänen, "It isn't ordinary, but because it is extraordinary, that way, that I believe that it didn't happen. Maybe you can recall to me that when it happened."

"Do you deny that this ever happened?" asked Donovan.

"I just asked, will you please tell me when it happened?" responded Häyhänen.

"If you can't even recall such an incident—" said Donovan.

"No, maybe I will recall at that time I was even in different city. That is what I would like to know."

* * *

Donovan moved on with his questioning of Häyhänen—this time to his drinking problem.

"At the time you lived in Bergen Street, did you drink?"

"Yes, I was drinking," confessed Häyhänen.

"How much?"

"In different days, different weeks, different way."

"What is the most you ever drank in one night while you were living at that address?" asked Donovan.

"About one pint," replied Häyhänen.

"Of what?" asked Donovan.

"A pint of vodka."

"Isn't it a fact that while you were living there, in Bergen Street, that you used to put out in the trash large quantities of liquor bottles? Isn't that true?"

The prosecutor interrupted with an objection, "What I would like to know is what Mr. Donovan calls large quantities of liquor bottles?"

Donovan responded, "A pint of vodka would be good enough for me, but I am just asking this question, your Honor."

The judge ruled, "I think that the witness is entitled to a rather definite suggestion. A large quantity of bottles over a long period of time would be one thing. A large quantity of bottles over a day or two would be another. Now, he is entitled to know what you are asking him about."

Donovan resumed his cross-examination of Häyhänen. "Didn't you at least once a week put out into your trash four or five whisky bottles or other liquor bottles?"

"Sometimes I put them once a week. Sometimes I put them once in three weeks. Because there are four rooms and big store-room there, is enough hiding place where I could put those empty bottles."

Donovan then asked, "And with an ambulance being called, attended by the police because of this wound on your leg, at this time we are to believe that you are a lieutenant colonel in the Soviet secret intelligence and that you were there to conduct an espionage cover operation, is that right?"

The prosecutor instantly objected, "Wait just a minute. I think the question is argumentative."

The judge replied, "It certainly is argumentative and recita-tive. If he answered a plain question: 'What was your position in the year 1953?' That would save time and trouble. Do you wish to ask that?"

Donovan responded, "No, your Honor."

"Now," said Donovan, "returning to the subject of drink, Mr. Häyhänen, do you still drink?"

"Yes."

"How much did you drink yesterday?"

"About four drinks as they serve in bars," said Häyhänen.

"Any alcohol this morning?"

"No."

The prosecutor objected. "I still, your Honor, don't see the materiality of this line of questioning in a conspiracy to commit espionage."

The judge replied, "It may go to the credibility of the witness."

Donovan closed his cross-examination by reading to the jury a handwritten statement signed by Häyhänen that read: "I resided and worked inland from July of 1949 to October of 1952. There I received my American passport and arrived to New York in October of 1952. I did not engage in espionage activity and did not receive any espionage or secret information from anyone during my stay abroad, neither in Finland nor in the United States of America."

"No further questions, your Honor," said Donovan.

CHAPTER TEN

The government called Sergeant Roy Rhodes to the witness stand, and his testimony proceeded as planned. Rhodes had worked as a mechanic in the motor pool at the US Embassy in Moscow, had an affair with a young party member, started sending sensitive information to the Soviets in exchange for money, and, when transferred back to the states, promised to do more of the same. It was damaging testimony in that Abel was later asked to track down Rhodes.

Rhodes had a background and expertise in the secret coding of US military documents. The KGB was also under the impression that Rhodes had relatives working in atomic weapons facilities, which the Soviets thought would be useful to their cause. The KGB wanted Abel to find Rhodes, who went by the code name "Quebec," and he gave Häyhänen the assignment. Häyhänen tried, but to no avail. The assignment, however, was important in Abel's trial because it was further proof that Abel was, in fact, a Soviet spy.

The prosecutor asked Häyhänen on the stand, "Between the time you first met 'Mark'—I believe you said July or August, 1954—and the time in June, 1955, when he left for Moscow, did 'Mark' give you any assignments?"

"Yes, he gave many," replied Häyhänen.

"Will you tell me about one of those assignments?"

Häyhänen replied, "One assignment, 'Mark' got instructions from Moscow to locate one illegal agent. And in that message was that his wife has three garages in Red Bank, and we made trip to Red Bank but we couldn't locate."

"Do you remember approximately when you made this trip to Red Bank with 'Mark'?" asked Thompson.

"We made that trip in the end of 1954."

"In other words, around November or December, 1954?"

"Yes, I believe in November, 1954."

"Do you know the name of the individual whom you were seeking information about?"

"Yes, I know," said Häyhänen.

"What was his name?"

"Roy Rhodes, and his nickname as agent was 'Quebec.'"

"When did you first hear the name 'Quebec?'" asked the prosecutor.

"When we made that trip to Red Bank, and we couldn't locate, so 'Mark' told that we have to ask for more instructions for more information about his relatives, or how to locate him because we couldn't locate him in Red Bank."

"Did you, pursuant to the conversation with 'Mark' about further instructions, did you seek further instructions?"

"Yes," said Häyhänen, "I had to send a message to Moscow, and in the same message, 'Mark' told that I may as well ask for more information about 'Quebec.' And then I had I got an answer to that message that 'Quebec's' relatives live in Colorado. And then 'Mark' gave me assignment to go to Colorado. And in Moscow's instructions there was that we have to make plan how to locate through his relatives that agent."

"Then you had a conversation with 'Mark' about the Colorado trip?"

"That's right," confirmed Häyhänen.

"Did he instruct you to go to Colorado?"

"Yes, sir."

"And did you go to Colorado?"

"Yes, I did."

"Whereabouts in Colorado did you go?"

Häyhänen replied, "To Salida. I was talking with 'Quebec's' sister by the phone, and she gave me 'Quebec's' mail address."

"When you got back to New York City, did you advise 'Mark' of the results of your trip?"

"On next meeting, it was several days later with 'Mark,' we have been talking about that trip, and he was satisfied that I found 'Quebec's' mail address, that 'Quebec' lived that time in Tucson, Arizona," said Häyhänen.

"Who paid for this trip?"

"'Mark' gave me money, and it was like trip expenses."

"As I understand, you reported to 'Mark' when you came back that you located Rhodes in Tucson, Arizona?"

"That's right," said Häyhänen.

"Did you discuss 'Quebec' further?"

"Yes," said Häyhänen, "We been discussing that it is, after all, too far to meet him each and to have some meeting places over there—that it will take long time. And 'Mark' told that because he has some other agents, and he cannot go for so long trip that I have to locate 'Quebec.'"

The prosecutor continued. "Now, did 'Mark' tell you in any conversation the reason for locating 'Quebec?'"

"Yes," replied Häyhänen, "then, before going to that Colorado trip he gave me a message on film where was more information about 'Quebec.' There was his nickname, his real name, then when he was born and where he was working, and who his parents and relatives are."

"Now, was that message on film?"

"Yes."

"What kind of film?" asked the prosecutor.

"It was ordinary 35-millimeter film, but later then I made soft film from it."

"In other words, it was hard film when you got it?"

"Yes."

"And you made it into soft film?"

"That's right."

The prosecutor queried, "How did you do that?"

"I did it by putting it to dioxane and after several hours it became soft film."

"Now, did 'Mark' tell you the reason that he wanted you to try and find Rhodes?"

"Yes," replied Häyhänen, "He told that he got instructions to locate him. But then, when I located him in Tucson, Arizona, he told that he cannot go over there, that I have to locate him."

"If 'Mark' discussed the purpose of locating Rhodes, what did he say to you?" asked the prosecutor.

"He said that 'Quebec' could be good agent because some of his relatives are working on military lands. He meant 'Quebec's' brother, who was working somewhere I cannot remember exactly, but in some atomic plant, or what it was."

The prosecutor resumed his questioning. "Mr. Häyhänen, you testified that you had received, as I recall, some information from 'Mark' relative to 'Quebec,' is that correct?"

"That's right, yes."

"And that you subsequently transferred it from hard film to soft film?"

"That's right," confirmed Häyhänen.

"Now, this message that you have just recognized, and which you say you transferred from hard film to soft film, what did you do with that message?"

"I put it into bolt."

"You put it into a bolt?"

"Yes, into container," said Häyhänen.

"Where did you put the container, if you remember?"

"I left that container, with some other bolts, in one of my rooms in Peekskill."

The prosecutor said, "Did you have any further conversations with the defendant relating to this 'Quebec,' Roy Rhodes?"

"Yes. We had several conversations about 'Quebec.'"

"Will you tell us about those conversations?"

"The conversation been that 'Mark' told that he may as well locate 'Quebec' himself on the way to Moscow," said Häyhänen.

"Did you have any other conversations about 'Quebec?'"

"Yes, then after 'Mark' returned from Moscow he explained that he didn't locate 'Quebec.'"

"Did you do anything further in an endeavor to locate 'Quebec?'" asked the prosecutor.

"No," said Häyhänen.

* * *

The cross-examination of Roy Rhodes by James Donovan was nothing if not predictable. Donovan would show the jury that Rhodes had never even met Abel, much less worked for him.

Donovan briskly walked to the front of the courtroom and announced, "May it please the court, would the defendant rise?" And Abel promptly stood up from his chair at the counsel table.

Donovan then directed his first question to Rhodes, "Sergeant Rhodes, have you ever seen this man before?"

"No, sir," answered Rhodes.

"Do you recognize him as anyone you have ever known under any name?"

"No, sir."

Donovan continued, "Do you know a man named 'Rudolf Abel?'"

"No, sir."

"Do you know a man named 'Emil Goldfus?'"

"No, sir."

"Do you know a man named 'Martin Collins?'"

"No, sir."

"Do you know a man named Reino Häyhänen, also known as 'Vic?'"

"No, sir."

"Do you know a man named 'Eugene Maki?'"

"No, sir."

"Do you know a man named 'Mikhail Svirin?'"

"No, sir."

"Do you know a man named 'Vitali G. Pavlov?'"

"I don't think so. No, sir."

"Do you know a man named 'Alexander M. Korotkin?'"

"No, sir."

"Do you know a man named 'Korotkov?'"

"No, sir."

Donovan then asked, "Have you ever had any representative of Soviet Russia communicate personally with you in the United States?"

"No, sir, not to my knowledge."

"In the United States, did you ever transmit to any Russian information concerning the national defense of the United States?"

"No, sir," replied Rhodes.

"Did you in the United States ever receive any such information for any Russian?"

"No, sir."

"Now, yesterday, Sergeant, you testified concerning transmitting information to Russian officials while you were stationed in Moscow. Is that correct?"

"Yes, sir."

Donavan dug deeper. "Did you at the time make any report on these treasonable activities to your superior officer?"

"No, sir," replied Rhodes.

"Did you make any report on these activities to any American official?"

"No, sir."

"What was the first time you admitted these activities to any official of the United States?"

146

"To the FBI in last of June, I believe, of this year," said Rhodes.

"Now, yesterday, Sergeant, as I understood you, you testified that your first meeting with that Russian girl occurred after you were celebrating the expected arrival of your wife and daughter in Russia, is that correct?"

Rhodes replied, "That is the way I can recall it, yes, sir."

"Now, is it not true that long after your family arrived in Moscow, that you attended a party in a hotel in Moscow at which uniformed Russians were present?"

"I did, yes, sir."

"Is it not a fact, sir, that subsequently that same evening that you found yourself in bed with a girl?" asked Donovan.

"I found myself alone with her, yes, sir. I don't recall finding myself in bed with her, no, sir."

Donovan had now caught Rhodes in a lie. "Would it help to refresh your recollection if I read to you the statement signed by you on July 2, 1957, and given to the FBI, which says, in part: 'At this party in the hotel room we also ate and drank, and I proceeded to get drunk. I remember that someone in the party had a girl brought in, and I was talking to her. I am very hazy on what took place, but recall at one time in the evening everybody had evidently left the room, and I found myself alone on the bed with this girl.'"

"That is true, I believe," confessed Rhodes.

"Now, this is after your wife and daughter had arrived in Moscow?" asked Donovan.

"That's right," said Rhodes.

Donovan proceeded. "Now, while you were in Moscow attached to the American Embassy, did you frequently drink intoxicating liquors?"

"I did, yes, sir."

"What liquor?"

"Whisky, vodka, almost anything we could get."

"In what quantities would you drink these liquors?"

"They weren't moderate," replied Rhodes.

"While attached to the American Embassy in Moscow for service as a United States master sergeant, is it not true that for the last two months of your stay in Moscow you were drunk every day?"

Rhodes confessed, "I believe that is right, yes, sir."

"Now, you testified yesterday, Sergeant, that during the period of time you were selling information to the Russians, that you received in return between $2,500 and $3,000?"

Toward the end of his cross-examination, Donovan asked, "Did you ever hear of a man named Benedict Arnold?"

"Yes, sir."

"How does he stay in your mind as an American in history?"

"Not so good," said Rhodes.

"Why?" asked Donovan.

"Isn't it because he betrayed his country?" continued Donovan.

"I think so," responded Rhodes.

"Do you know enough history to know that even Benedict Arnold didn't do it for money?" inquired Donovan.

"I know it," replied Rhodes.

Donovan then announced to the court, "Sergeant, Benedict Arnold may have been the greatest traitor in American military history, but it was only until today."

The judge asked, "Is that a question?"

Donovan replied, "It is an attempted statement of fact."

The prosecutor then said, "Your Honor, I think Mr. Donovan will agree with me that the last statement of his should properly be stricken from the record."

Donovan replied, "I didn't want to make it in the record, your Honor. I just wanted to make it."

The court responded, "You had the satisfaction of making it. Now, are you willing that it be stricken from the record?"

"Very well," said Donovan.

The witness Roy Rhodes, at long last, was excused from the witness stand.

CHAPTER ELEVEN

As he looked in the mirror that morning, Donovan knew the battle to save his client from the electric chair was an uphill one, and that the situation was dire. Abel had not taken the witness stand to defend himself, and the government had levied an effective barrage of evidence against him.

Donovan's closing argument was as good as they get under the circumstances. He knew he would have to show the jury the lack of direct evidence relating to Abel's espionage activities, he knew he would have to convince them of the bravery of his client in serving his own country on a dangerous mission, and he knew that he must remind them of the extremely seedy character of Reino Häyhänen and Roy Rhodes as the state's primary witnesses. But most importantly, he had to persuade the jury that the trial was not about punishing Communism and the infiltration of a foreign enemy onto the shores of America.

It was a very tall order.

The judge called the court to order and invited Donovan to make his closing argument. Donovan slowly rose from his wooden chair, circled around the counsel's table, and walked to the front of the courtroom.

"May it please the court; ladies and gentleman of the jury: This trial has been an experience for me, and I am sure for you as well.

All experiences are meaningful when we look at them with the benefit of hindsight.

"When this trial commenced, I spoke briefly to you about your duty as a juror. I explained that your duty is to determine the facts and find whether this man named Abel has been proved guilty of the specific charges against him by the evidence produced. I explained that this is not a trial of Communism, and it is not a trial of Soviet Russia.

"We have now seen all the evidence. We had an opportunity to evaluate the witnesses to see whether or not they were telling the truth, and what their motives were to tell the truth, or what their motives were to tell whatever story would save their own skins.

"It is terribly important in this particular trial that you have a clear concept of the function of the jury. We believe that our trial by jury system is the best system ever devised for arriving at the truth.

"Why is your function so important? You might say to yourselves, 'The judge knows all the law applicable to the case. He has been trained for years to evaluate evidence. Why shouldn't cases such as this be left to the lawyers and the judges?'

"The answer is that from the time of Aristotle, ordinary citizens are not content to leave these questions to the lawyers and the judges with their legalisms and legal niceties.

"All that I am going to ask you to do in this particular case is use your common sense. You are the only people in this courtroom who can come back with a verdict of guilty or not guilty on each count. I ask you to review what we have listened to the last couple of weeks and use common sense in reaching your verdict.

"As you know, there are three counts in the indictment. The heart of the indictment is that this man 'did unlawfully, willfully, and knowingly conspire to communicate, deliver, and transmit to a foreign government, to wit, the Union of Soviet Socialist Republics, and representatives and agents thereof, directly and indirectly, documents, writings, photographs, photographic negatives, plans, maps, models, notes, instruments, appliances, and information relating to the national defense of the United States of America, and particularly information relating to arms, equipment, and disposition of United States Armed Forces, and information relating to the atomic energy program of the United States.'

"This is the charge.

"Count one is the only capital count. It charges a conspiracy to transmit national defense information and atomic energy information. I ask you this right now because I am going to be asking it repeatedly as I go through this case: What evidence of national defense or atomic information has been put before you?

"Certainly we expected evidence that this man stole great military secrets, secrets of atomic energy, and so on. Looking back over the past couple of weeks, what evidence of such information was ever produced?

"Remember that it is essential for you to be able to say that this man has been proved guilty beyond a reasonable doubt of a conspiracy to transmit such information. The only reason why this particular conspiracy is punishable by death is because it is a conspiracy to transmit military information affecting the national defense.

"The second count of this indictment deals with gathering such information in a conspiracy. The first count is a conspiracy to transmit such information. The second count is a conspiracy to gather such information. The third count deals with failure to register in the United States as an agent of Soviet Russia.

"Remember that the indictment is not evidence. It was only handed up after one side was heard without cross-examination. Remember that until the man is proven guilty he is innocent.

"Before I review this evidence, I want briefly to ask you one common sense question: Would you briefly compare the evidence that you have about this man, and then compare that evidence with what you know of his two principal accusers?

"In the first place, let's assume for the moment that the man is what the government says he is. It means that such a man was serving his country on an extraordinarily dangerous mission. In our armed forces, we only send on such missions the bravest, the most intelligent, men that we can find.

"Every American who took the witness stand in this case who personally knew the man while he was living here became a character witness for this defendant. You heard those men one after the other testify. Did they know anything about him? No.

"Meanwhile, yesterday afternoon, you heard the letters from the man's family. Obviously they painted the picture of a devout husband, a loving father. In short, an outstanding type of family man such as we have in the United States.

"So, on the one hand, you have a very brave patriotic man serving his country on an extraordinarily hazardous military mission, and who lived among us in peace during these years. And, on the other hand, you have the two people that you heard testify as his principal accusers.

"Häyhänen, a renegade by any measure. A bum. A liar. A thief. You could just run down the adjectives to describe such a man. He was followed by the only soldier in American history who has ever confessed to selling out his country for money.

"These are the two principal witnesses against this man. Let's turn in more detail to this man who said that his name was Reino Häyhänen. If what the government says is true, the man was trained to live a life of deception. He is a trained liar who was being paid by Russia to live that life, so he is a professional liar. And now, as you know, he is being paid by our government.

"The prosecutor will tell you that it is necessary to use such witnesses. However, I ask you to question whether he is telling the truth or whether he is telling lies that may save his own skin.

"From the evidence before you I say that you should conclude that Häyhänen is a liar, a thief, and a bigamist who said he was on an undercover espionage operation.

"In Newark, New Jersey, between August 1953 and December 1954, this man did everything possible to attract attention. His said he leased that shop for a photographic studio. He stayed there a year and never opened a studio. He was living there with this Finnish lady, drinking vodka by the pint, and at least once the police and an ambulance were called because two of the rooms were splattered with blood.

"With respect to the Finnish lady, you heard me ask him whether he recalled an incident in the bakery next door where he bought a loaf of bread, then threw it on the floor and ordered the woman to pick it up. He couldn't recall such an incident. I specifically asked him, 'Do you deny that it occurred?' He never denied it. Never denied it.

"While this kind of a life was going on, you and I are being asked to believe that the man was a lieutenant colonel in Russian military intelligence. At one point, he admits that he left his wife and son in Russia because he seemed to prefer the Finnish lady. Let's assume not only the miserable character of this man, let's assume the sordid life he led here.

"You are left with the basic question: Assuming all that, is the man's basic story true? He was here for some reason. He used all of these fantastic methods of communicating with someone. At times he said he used these drops and hollowed-out bolts and so on to communicate with the defendant. One minute after he testified to that, he was telling you he met the defendant every week and they used to go for drives for an hour. If he met him every week and went for drives by the hour, what would be the object of communicating with him through these melodramatic, boyish devices?

"In addition to communicating with Abel, he used all of these devices to communicate with a group of nameless, faceless people whom he would only describe as 'Soviet officials.' They were never identified by name, rank, or any other description.

"We have examined hundreds and hundreds of pages of testimony in this case. In two places he was asked, 'Why did you come to America?' 'I came to America to help with espionage.' In another place he is asked, 'What kind of information were you trying to get,' and his answer was virtually out of the law book on the statute involved. He said it was to 'affect the national security of the United States.'

"Except for those two tiny threads spoken by as miserable a witness as you ever would put on the stand, there is no evidence pertaining to the national defense or atomic energy secrets. It is with that kind of evidence that you are being asked to send a man possibly to his death?

"Bear in mind the specific conspiracy charge. Let's review what this man Häyhänen says he did in furtherance of this conspiracy. He went out to Colorado to find a man whom he never met. He went down to Atlantic City to find another man that he never met. He went up to Quincy, Massachusetts, to locate another man, and to this day he is not sure that he found the right man.

"He was told he should open a photographic shop as a cover, and he never opened the shop. He was told to learn Morse code, and he never learned it. He was given money to give to Mrs. Sobell, but he never met up with her, and he pocketed the $5,000.

"If that man was a spy, history will certainly record that he is the most fumbling, self-defeating, inefficient spy a country ever sent. It is an incredible story, and we are to believe that this is a lieutenant colonel in Russian military intelligence sent here to obtain our highest defense secrets. That bum wouldn't have 'private first class' stripes in the American army.

"However, rather than dwell on that man's testimony, which I say proved absolutely nothing, I want to recall what is the most significant evidence the man gave. I asked him whether or not he had given this statement to the FBI in late May, in early June of 1957. He said he did. He said he gave it in a hotel room here in New York.

"Let me read this again to you very carefully and remember this is the government's own document. This is what the man told the FBI in late May and early June of this year: 'I resided and worked in Finland from July 1949 to October 1952. There I received my American passport and arrived in New York. I did not engage in espionage activity and did not receive any espionage or secret information from anyone during my stay abroad, neither in Finland nor in the United States of America.'

"This is the man's own statement to the FBI, made here in New York City in late May or early June of 1957.

"And it is on this man's testimony that you are supposed to convict a man of a capital offense. It is ridiculous. That statement was never cleared up on redirect examination. To this day, that statement remains in this case as the man's own testimony.

"It is a complete exculpation of this defendant, and no explanation of it has ever been offered. This is the principal thing you should remember when you think of Häyhänen's testimony as a witness.

"Now, what about the rest of the evidence? Sergeant Rhodes appeared. You all had an opportunity to see the type he was: dissolute, a drunkard, betraying his own country. Words can hardly describe the depths to which that man has fallen.

"Remember that Rhodes testified he never met or heard of Häyhänen or the defendant. Meanwhile, he told in detail here his own life in Moscow, selling us out for money. How is this related to this defendant?

"Those events in Moscow occurred two years before Häyhänen says Abel sent him to locate a man named Rhodes. How did these relate to this man? The answer is—they don't relate in any way. It is with evidence of that kind that you are being asked to convict this man.

"Where is the evidence of information relating to the national defense and of atomic energy? The answer is, if there is any such evidence, it has not been produced before you. If they had a case on it, it hasn't been made, and you have to pass on the evidence which has been put forward.

"I ask you to look at these decoded messages and see for yourselves whether they relate in any way to national defense information or atomic energy: 'Nobody came to meeting either eight or nine as I was advised he should. Why should he be inside or outside? Is time wrong? Place seems right. Please check.'

"I submit to you that on this evidence you could reasonably conclude that there is some kind of a conspiracy, but that isn't the question. It isn't a question of whether there has been some sort of conspiracy going on. The question is—did they prove this *specific* conspiracy?

"To do that, they must prove that it is a conspiracy to transmit and to gather national defense information, military secrets, atomic energy secrets, and things of that kind. There is no evidence in this case that that occurred.

"It is very important that you realize that in this case you are not serving your country and you are not fighting Communism to convict a man on insufficient evidence. You are only serving your country and fighting Communism if you bring in a just verdict.

"If, after this case is all over, you want to live with your neighbors and with yourselves, you must exercise your consciences to reach a just verdict. Ladies and gentlemen of the jury, I ask you to exercise your individual consciences as to whether or not this man was proved to be guilty beyond a reasonable doubt of the specific crimes charged.

"As you deliberate this question, ask yourselves one final question: Where was the information affecting the national defense of the United States? If you will resolve this case on that higher level, you can leave it with a clear conscience.

"Certainly, on counts one and two in this indictment, you must bring in a verdict of not guilty. Thank you."

In the end, James Donovan may have gone too far in calling Rudolf Abel "a brave patriot who was serving his country." In a time when the Soviet threat was real, this may have antagonized the jury. And if Abel was a hero, wasn't Häyhänen—who was doing the same thing—also one?

The jury could see that Häyhänen had a drinking and a domestic abuse problem, but alcoholics and wife-beaters are capable of telling the truth. And one could hardly blame Häyhänen for defecting when it looked like he was about to be banished to Siberia—or worse.

And likewise for Roy Rhodes. He, too, had a drinking problem and had succumbed to filthy lucre in exchange for money from the Soviets. And as despicable as that was, the jury no doubt could see that it was a mechanic who worked at an embassy. How much could he really reveal?

And as for Abel, he wouldn't take the stand to defend himself. It was obvious he had nothing to say. Especially with truckloads of incriminating evidence taken out of his hotel room and studio.

Donovan did the best he could with what he had, but as he took his seat, he somehow knew that his client did not stand a chance.

CHAPTER TWELVE

The judge indicated to the prosecutor that it was time to give his closing argument for the government. The prosecutor walked to the front of the jury box, hesitated for a moment, and then began.

"May it please the court; ladies and gentlemen of the jury: Before I get into my summation, I certainly want to thank you for your patience and the courtesy that you have shown to counsel on both sides. There have been some trying days, but you have been more than patient, and I am most appreciative.

"In my opening I think I made a solemn promise to you that the government would do everything to afford this defendant a fair trial, and I believe we have conducted ourselves that way. I further pointed out that it wasn't the government's aim to simply win a case, but of far greater importance was that justice be done. In other words, that innocence not suffer, nor guilt escape.

"You are going to hear me use the terms 'undisputed' and 'uncontradicted' many times, because I can think of no substantial fact that the government has presented to you that has been contradicted.

"I want to talk very briefly about conspiracy. In my opening I said simply that it is a partnership in crime, and that the accomplishment of one overt act completes it. It need not be successful to be a crime. Let me use a simple example: If two people agree

159

to assassinate the president and one of them procured a gun, that would be all that you need to complete the crime, and it need not be completed to be a crime.

"In other words, we don't have to stand idly by until you have a corpse on your hands. And that is this case. We don't have to stand idly by and permit an individual to commit espionage. We are not powerless. We may intervene. We may prevent the consummation of the crime.

"I want to talk briefly about Reino Häyhänen, who was referred to this morning as a trained liar. In my opening, I think I told you that you could expect an attack, and you got it: 'a trained liar; a professional liar. Trained liar.'

"The same training as the defendant, but less time in the NKVD. Häyhänen, 'a trained liar;' the defendant, 'a brave, patriotic man serving his country on a hazardous mission.' And, believe me, we intend to make that type of mission very hazardous. He is a good family man, and his family is living very well in Moscow with a summer home and servants.

"Reino Häyhänen testified, and was subject to cross-examination for four days. Defense counsel suggested you watch his demeanor, and I certainly hope you watched how readily he answered the questions. He admitted that he drank. He admitted that he took Mrs. Sobell's $5,000, and nobody condones that. I don't recall him admitting, however, throwing a loaf of bread on a bakery floor.

"Häyhänen testified that in 1939 he was drafted into the NKVD. He testified that he had been educated in the local schools and teacher's college, and that his work in the NKVD from 1939 to 1948 consisted mainly of counterespionage. He testified that he had been trained in the use of weapons and how to conduct surveillances. He had been checking on Russian nationals. And in 1948 he was called to Moscow and reassigned to espionage work. "Where? In the United States. In preparation for that assignment he received further training from 1948 to 1952. You recall that while he was in Moscow he met a man named Svirin. The next time he saw Svirin it was at the Prospect Park subway station in New York City.

"Häyhänen testified that the purpose of his coming to the United States was to procure secret information, military or atomic. When he arrived here in 1952, Häyhänen was a trained, skilled espionage agent. Thirteen years of experience in the use of weapons, surveillance, and microdot training.

"He was trained in the English language and in the use of radio, secret message containers, and false documents. When he left Finland for the United States, he was given the location of drops that were used to communicate with other members of the conspiracy.

"In 1954, he met the defendant and subsequently performed certain assignments for the defendant. He talked about an endeavor to locate a soldier, Roy Rhodes, in Red Bank, New Jersey. He then had another assignment up in the Boston area to locate a Swedish individual. He went to Atlantic City with the defendant to locate another individual. At the direction of the defendant, he then went to Queens to surveil an individual there. Before the defendant went to Moscow, he instructed Häyhänen to set up a photographic studio in Newark.

"It was stated that Roy Rhodes was an accuser. Rhodes was nothing of the sort. Rhodes testified that he did not know Häyhänen or Abel. But Abel knew about Rhodes, and so did Häyhänen. The government has an obligation to present evidence to prove the truth of the charge of the grand jury.

"We are not proud of Roy Rhodes. Nobody could be. He is an admitted espionage agent. We simply presented Rhodes to corroborate the 'Quebec' message; and his testimony coincided with items contained in the 'Quebec' message, which the defendant had given to Häyhänen, and items that Rhodes admitted he had given to Russian officials in Moscow.

"The government showed that Rhodes had furnished the Russians with information while he was there. The government showed that he had been paid for that information. In other words, the defense discredited an already discredited witness. But the important thing is that his testimony about the information he furnished to the Russians was never contradicted.

"Abel wasn't seeking decent citizens. He was seeking people like Roy Rhodes, because decent citizens can be of no help to a Soviet conspiracy, but a compromised army sergeant who has previously furnished information to the Soviets can. You give a Soviet agent an opportunity to get the background and the connections of any individual in the military and you have given him a lot to start from.

"I can't think of anyone better than Rhodes to get military information relating to our national defense. Rhodes had been trained in code work, and he had so advised the Russians. The 'Quebec' message revealed that the Russians thought that he had a brother working in an atomic plant.

"I have mentioned the trip to Moscow. Reino Häyhänen said that the defendant had taken a trip to Moscow. Can that be corroborated? Harry McMullen, the superintendent at 252 Fulton Street, testified that the defendant was away for about the last five months of 1955. We checked the rent payments. We checked the bank deposit and withdrawal records. Then, you recall the letter from his daughter in January 1956 that showed her father had recently been home.

"The Prospect Park bolt is also strong corroboration of the testimony of Reino Häyhänen. You recall that Häyhänen said that he had noticed that the drop in Prospect Park had been cemented over. That location was divulged to the FBI. You heard the testimony of the FBI agent going to that location, finding it, chipping away the cement, and finding the bolt. You heard the FBI agent testify that when he opened the bolt there was a typed message inside.

"Which brings me to one of the most important items of proof in the case—the typewriter. Who placed a typewriter in Abel's possession? One of the defendant's character witnesses. And you heard special agent Webb testify to the typewriter examination.

"Who do you think was using the drops in Prospect Park for messages? The defendant. You heard Webb testify that the message contained in the Prospect Park bolt had been typed on the typewriter that belonged to the defendant. What other collaboration was there concerning the typewriter? Mr. Tribelhorn testified he received a letter from the defendant. Mr. Webb said the letter had also been typed on the defendant's typewriter. I think this is overwhelming proof.

"You will recall that a seventeen-year-old newsboy came in here and testified that in June 1953 he dropped a nickel he got in change and that it came open. The boy immediately turned it over to a Brooklyn police detective, who turned it over to the FBI. The message was dated December 1952, and it contained congratulations on a safe arrival. Remember that Häyhänen arrived here in October 1952. The message said, 'We have sent $3,000.' You recall Häyhänen's testimony that he had requested money, and that under that lamppost in Fort Tryon Park, he had picked up $3,000.

"You will recall that Häyhänen testified that the defendant said he was going away at the end of April because his sinuses bothered him. He paid two months' rent in advance to McMullen and left. After that, McMullen didn't see him around, and some of his character witnesses didn't see him around, either.

"However, there were two FBI agents on the top floor of the Touraine Hotel who saw him. The FBI's surveillance placed the defendant, strangely enough, in the studio at 252 Fulton Street on May 23, at 10:45 p.m.. He left at 11:50 p.m.. It is quite a coincidence that those periods in the studio coincide with the radio schedule found in the Hotel Latham where he was staying. Then, on June 13th, the FBI agents placed the defendant in the studio at 252

Fulton Street, from a period of ten o'clock to 11:50 p.m.. It happens to coincide with the radio schedule again.

"I mention this because of the independent corroboration of Häyhänen's testimony, which we promised you. I don't find the substance of his testimony contradicted, disputed, or challenged.

"Who was he corroborated by? The thirteen FBI agents who did a magnificent job in a very difficult case. Thirteen of them. You saw them, and you saw their demeanor on the stand, and you are able to evaluate their testimony, the careful, painstaking work of a great organization. Corroboration by thirteen plain American citizens with no interest except that justice be done.

"And then, of course, you recall that Häyhänen said he had gotten some spectroscopic film from the defendant, and I think it was clearly shown to you the availability of this type of film. It wasn't developed by the government. You heard the Eastman Kodak witness state that of all types of spectroscopic film, that there has only been one sale in the last five years, and it was made to, strangely enough, 'E. R. Goldfus.' Very strange.

"What about items that Häyhänen didn't know anything about that could inculpate this defendant? Look at them. These are out of the storeroom over at 252 Fulton Street: a hollow tie clasp, a hollow cuff link, a hollow bolt, a hollow battery. Häyhänen never saw this, never knew of its existence. These items have been referred to as toys. They are not toys for amusement. They are tools for the destruction of our country, which is the purpose of this conspiracy.

"Now, let's talk a little bit about the conduct of the defendant. There isn't anyone who knew him as Rudolph Abel. He was known as 'Goldfus,' known as 'Mark,' and known as 'Martin Collins.' Not one of his character witnesses knew him as Rudolph Abel.

"His conduct can best be described as secretive and intended to deceive, showing the cunning of a professional, a highly trained espionage agent, a master spy, a real pro. This was the man's chosen career. He knows the rules of this game, and so does his family. He is entitled to no sympathy.

"Let's talk a minute also about the items that were found without Häyhänen or Rhodes, who have been labeled the two chief accusers. The typewriter, birth certificates, and the tie clasp and cuff links. How about the hollow pencil? This pencil was thrown in the wastepaper basket in the Latham Hotel. How about the code book, concealed in a sanding block, which you saw yesterday?

"Reino Häyhänen didn't slip that into the defendant's possession. Or the nickel message in the Prospect Park drop and the radio schedule. How about the defendant's own admissions in McAllen, Texas, that he was a citizen of the USSR? He hasn't informed the United States Attorney General of his address, that he is in this country illegally, and that he has concealed his identity. What could be more cogent?

"Let's get back to the evidence. At the end of April of this year, he told Harry McMullen that he was going away for his sinus trouble. He also told Levine, one of his character witnesses, that he was going away. For the first time, the defendant paid two months' rent in advance to McMullen. Where did he go on vacation for that sinus trouble? He went across the river to the Broadway Central Hotel. I don't know what Manhattan has got for treatment of sinus conditions that Brooklyn doesn't have, but that is where he went.

"And for the first time, he uses the name 'Martin Collins.' About this time, Häyhänen had left, ostensibly for Moscow. Could there be any question on the identity of 'Martin Collins'? When he registered at the Broadway Central, he put as a contact Ben Silverman, 252 Fulton Street. He then left the Broadway Central Hotel. Where did he go? He went to Daytona Beach, Florida, where he again registered as 'Martin Collins.' After leaving Daytona Beach, he registered on May 18th at the Latham Hotel as 'Martin Collins.' He stayed there until June 21st, and during this very shaky period he procured an international certificate of vaccination.

"You will recall that he was never seen back at the studio by any of his character witnesses. He was never seen by the building superintendent. The only people who saw him were the vigilant FBI agents who were surveilling the studio. They saw him on evenings and at times that coincide completely with the radio schedule that was in the pencil that he threw in the wastepaper basket at the Latham.

"Never in my experience have I seen such overwhelming corroboration. We promised we would give you direct evidence, and we did. We said there would be circumstantial evidence, and you got it. We said there would be documentary evidence, and we produced it. We said we would prove through admissions of the defendant that he was guilty of the offense charged.

"This is a serious case, and this is a serious offense. This is an offense directed at the very existence of the free world and civilization itself. And I am convinced that the government has proven its case not only beyond a reasonable doubt, but beyond all possible doubt. I am convinced that you in your wisdom and judgment will be able to evaluate the truth of the various witnesses the government has presented. I am sure that you will arrive at the correct result.

"I can't stress too strongly that a person doesn't have to succeed in a conspiracy to be guilty of it. A society and its government are entitled to protect itself when they find people conspiring to commit an offense. We are not helpless. We don't have to wait until the corpse is on the ground before we can move in. We can move in as soon as the crime has been accomplished.

"In closing, I want to say that we appreciate your courtesy and the attention you have paid to this very important case. I am convinced that after you have considered everything, you will find this defendant guilty by the overwhelming weight of the evidence that the government has presented."

The prosecutor's argument was very effective. It emphasized the seriousness of the offense and admitted liabilities of Rhodes.

It pointed out that Abel and Häyhänen were doing exactly the same thing, but that Donavan had called one a hero and the other a scoundrel. But the most important line was the one that the government doesn't have to wait until the espionage crime is completed to apprehend the spy. This took the wind out of the sails of the defendant that there was no direct evidence of espionage. The jury could see the mounds of spy equipment activities and assume that they were being used for nefarious purpose.

CHAPTER THIRTEEN

On November 15, 1957, the court was ready to present its charge, and the judge announced to the jury its responsibilities.

"Members of the jury, the time has now come for you to take over your deliberations in this case. Doubtless you feel that you know a great deal about it, and perhaps you prefer not to have to listen to anything from the court on the subject. If that is your point of view, it is also mine, but we cannot yield to our preferences. It is my duty to give a charge, and it is your duty to listen to it."

The court then laid out the elements of each count of the indictment.

* * *

The clerk of the court called out, "Rudolf I. Abel, for sentence." His attorney Donovan replied, "Ready, sir."

The judge then asked, "Is there something to be said before the imposition of sentence, either on the part of the defendant or the government?"

Donovan stated, "Your Honor, I addressed a letter to your Honor yesterday which was delivered this morning, and I would appreciate it if I could read that letter into the record." The judge agreed, "Surely."

Mr. Donovan read the letter:

My dear Judge Byers:

On November 15, 1957, the defendant in this case will appear before the court for sentencing. While I shall request the privilege of making a brief oral statement on behalf of the defendant at that time, this letter is addressed to the court beforehand so that there may be adequate opportunity for the court and the government to consider the substance of the statements which I shall make at the time of sentence.

The defendant has been convicted on all three counts of the indictment. Count number one carries a penalty of death and imprisonment for any term of years or for life. Count number two carries a penalty of a fine of not more than $10,000, or imprisonment for not more than ten years, or both. Count number three carries a penalty of a fine of not more than $10,000, imprisonment for not more than five years, or both.

The following arguments are predicated upon the assumption that the defendant has been found guilty of these offenses in accordance with all provisions of law.

First, it will be my contention that the interests of justice and the national interests of the United States dictate that the death penalty should not be considered. This is because:

(a) No evidence was introduced by the government to show that the defendant actually gathered or transmitted any information pertaining to the national defense;

(b) Normal justification of the death penalty is its possible effect as a deterrent; it is absurd to believe that the execution of this man would deter the Russian military;

(c) The effect of imposing the death penalty upon a foreign national, for a peacetime conspiracy to commit espionage, should be weighed by the government with respect to the activities of our own citizens abroad;

(d) To date, the government has not received from the defendant what it would regard as "cooperation." However, it of course remains possible that in the event of various contingencies this situation would be altered in the future, and

accordingly it would appear to be in the national interest to keep the man available for a reasonable period of time; (e) It is possible that in the foreseeable future an American of equivalent rank will be captured by Soviet Russia or ally of Russia. At such time the exchange of prisoners through diplomatic channels could be considered to be in the best national interest of the United States.

With respect to an appropriate term of years, the following facts are submitted as pertinent because this problem is novel in American jurisprudence:

(a) During the 1920s, when France was the strongest power on the European continent and hence a primary objective of Soviet espionage, the average sentence given by the French courts to Soviet agents convicted of actually acquiring defense information was three years imprisonment; (b) The sole British statute applicable to a similar case, of peacetime espionage by an alien, is the Official Secrets Act, first passed in 1889, with a maximum penalty of life imprisonment; repealed and reenacted in 1911 with a maximum penalty of seven years; increased to fourteen years in 1920.

Before writing this letter, I sought and obtained the opportunity to discuss the matter in Washington with various interested government departments and agencies, including the Department of Justice. This does not mean that any one of such parties necessarily concurs in the foregoing.

Very truly yours,

(Signed) James B. Donovan

Donovan continued, "To that, your Honor, I would only add that the defendant Abel is a man fifty-five years old. He has faithfully served his country. Whether that country is right or wrong, it is his country, and I ask only that the court consider that we are legally at peace with that country. I ask that the judgment of the court be based on logic and justice tempered with mercy."

The judge then asked, "Does the defendant wish to be heard on his own behalf?"

Abel meekly answered, "No, I have nothing to say, your Honor."

The judge then turned to the prosecutor, "Mister prosecutor, has the government anything to say?"

The prosecutor responded, "If your Honor pleases, the imposition of sentence is, of course, wholly a matter within your Honor's discretion. However, it may be of some aid and assistance to the court in reaching its determination to have the benefit of the government's observations and comments as to some of the matters which the court would normally take into consideration in imposing sentence.

"First, just a word or two about the defendant himself: He is not a novice in the field of espionage. By training and by profession, for a period of over thirty years, he has been an agent for espionage. He entered this country, by his own admission, in 1948, by stealth, employing a fictitious name, a phony passport, and a cunning which his training as a Soviet intelligence officer had given him. For the next nine years, by his own admission, he concealed his presence in this country by hiding his true identity from all with whom he came in contact.

"During his residence in the United States, he is known to have communicated directly and indirectly with Moscow, and to have received instructions and to have activated agents and built an espionage apparatus. The extent of Abel's activities are well known to the court from the evidence presented at the trial, and I am not going to go into the evidence any further because your Honor is so familiar with it.

"There are, of course, many approaches to sentencing. The deterrent effect which the sentence will have on others, rehabilitation, and retribution. The concepts of rehabilitation or retribution would appear to have little application to this case, and I certainly think it would be naive to assume that a substantial sentence would deter the Soviets from continuing their espionage operations directed at this country and at the free world. But it would certainly serve notice upon the men in the Soviet Union, in the Kremlin, and those who carry out their assignments, that the commission of espionage in the United States is a hazardous undertaking.

"The crime of which the defendant was convicted is not of the usual variety coming before this court. I might say that the crime which he stands convicted of is not the same crime that Mr. Donovan adverted to when he quoted Dallin and from the British Official Secrets Act of back in 1920 and back in 1911.

"Espionage in 1957, I think, is completely different. The threat against civilization, the threat against this country, and the whole free world is inherent in this crime. In other words, it is an offense against the whole American people rather than a few individuals. So the punishment should be commensurate with the magnitude of the offense.

"The present dangers which this country faces from the country whose leaders tell us, 'They will bury us,' must also be considered. While no shooting war exists, as Mr. Donovan has pointed out, no shooting war exists with the Soviets, we are engaged in a cold war with that country, the outcome of which could well decide who would be victorious in a hot war.

"In such circumstances, this government must deal drastically with agents of foreign power who cross our borders by subterfuge for the purpose of seeking out our vital national secrets.

"Now, in the light of all these factors and considerations, the government has certainly no hesitation in recommending, and indeed, it seems to me, has a duty of requesting, the imposition of a substantial and very strong sentence in this case."

* * *

The court concluded, "If there is nothing more to be said by either side, sentence will now be imposed. The question of the sentence in this case presents no particular problem concerning the defendant as an individual. The court knows next to nothing about his personal life or his true character, nor about the motives that may have caused him to enter this country illegally in 1948 and here conduct himself ever since as an undercover agent of the USSR for the purposes described in the testimony of his assistant and accomplice.

"Lacking this insight into the man known as Abel, the evidence requires that he be dealt with as one who chose his career with knowledge of its hazards and the price that he would have to pay in the event of detection and conviction of the violation of the laws of the United States enacted by Congress for the protection of the American people and our way of life.

"Thus, the problem will be seen to present the single question of how the defendant should be dealt with so that the interests of the United States in the present, and in the foreseeable future, are to be best served, so far as those interests can be reasonably forecast.

"Many considerations have been involved in that study. It would not be the part of wisdom to recite them in the record, but suffice it to say that in the measured judgment of this court, the following sentence, based upon the jury's verdict of guilty as to each count of the indictment, is believed to meet the test which has been stated.

"Pursuant to the verdict of guilty as to Count 1, the defendant is committed to the custody of the Attorney General of the United States tor imprisonment in a federal institution to be selected by him, for the period of thirty years.

"Pursuant to the same verdict as to Count 2, the defendant is committed to the custody of the Attorney General of the United States for imprisonment in federal institution to be selected by him for the period of ten years, plus a fine of $2,000, the defendant to stand committed for nonpayment of the fine.

"Pursuant to the same verdict as to Count 3, the defendant is committed to the custody of the Attorney General of the United States for imprisonment in a federal institution to be selected by him for the period of five years, plus a fine of $1,000, the defendant to stand committed for nonpayment of the said fine.

"The terms of imprisonment are concurrent. The fines are consecutive."

* * *

Abel had been convicted, but spared execution. Conspiracy to transmit atomic secrets—count one of the indictment—was a capital offense. Abel was instead sentenced to thirty years in an Atlanta penitentiary. Abel owed his life to his lawyer's foresight and skill in articulating the national interest in preserving Abel's life for an exchange of agents at some future date, even though it would be three years before the first spy swaps began.

CHAPTER FOURTEEN

As one would expect, Abel appealed his conviction to the Second Circuit Court of Appeals. The primary issue raised was whether the prohibition of unreasonable searches and seizures was violated when government agents, without a search warrant, searched Abel's hotel and seized the articles they found there.

The search-and-seizure issue raised several important legal issues. The appellate court held that government agents may, pursuant to a lawful arrest, conduct a search of the premises where the arrest is made. The attorneys for Abel argued that, in every case where such a search has been upheld, the arrest was made for the commission of a crime, but that the issuance of an *administrative* arrest warrant did not confer the same rights. The charges for which Abel was arrested could have been made the subject of either a criminal prosecution *or* a deportation hearing. Arrest and detention for deportation offenses are expressly allowed by statute.

Abel contended that the search conducted by the INS agents violated the Fourth Amendment, because the *true* objective of the arresting officers was to uncover evidence of espionage rather than to discover weapons or evidence of alienage. The argument was roundly rejected by the appellate judges. It was true, the court explained, that the INS first learned of Abel's illegal presence in this country from the FBI, but that fact alone did not necessarily indicate that the INS search was made in bad faith.

The head of INS testified that the agency's interest in Abel was limited to his illegal presence in the United States. This testimony was corroborated by the articles seized from Abel's room: (1) the 'Martin Collins' birth certificate, (2) the 'Emil Goldfus' birth certificate, (3) the international certificate of vaccination in the name of 'Martin Collins,' and (4) a bank book issued by the East River Savings Bank to 'E. R. Goldfus.' The seizure of these four items was clearly consistent with a search intended to obtain evidence of alienage. The seizure of the slips of paper that Abel attempted to hide in his shirt sleeves occurred only after Abel tried to conceal them, and it was obvious that they were the instrumentalities by which he might commit the crime of espionage.

The appellate court also found that the record contained more than enough evidence that Abel conspired with others to act on behalf of the Soviet government. Abel argued that the evidence did not support the government charges showing the conspiracy's purpose was to gather and transmit to the USSR information relating to the national defense of the United States. Abel pointed out that there was no evidence showing that he ever *succeeded* in communicating any information other than the type which could lawfully be sent abroad.

The court conceded there was not the slightest hint that these espionage agents met with any success. However, Abel was convicted of having *conspired* with others to gather and transmit secret information pertaining to the national defense of the United States, and the record was clear that Abel knew of the unlawful purpose of this conspiracy. In other words, a conspirator's lack of success does not mitigate the criminality of his activities.

Häyhänen had testified to a sequence of events that not only proved the purpose of the conspiracy, but the fact that Abel was fully aware of the conspiracy's purpose. The jury was justified in inferring that Abel and his co-conspirators were interested in establishing contact with another Soviet agent named Roy Rhodes, who was supposedly a valuable source of information about atomic bombs.

The jury was no doubt impressed by the elaborate precautions taken by the conspirators to keep their activities secret. The court noted that individuals intent on gathering public information do not find it necessary to employ secret codes, microdots, hollowed-out coins, and drop-off points for cryptic messages. The use of such methods was sufficient to justify the jury's finding that the object of the conspiracy was to transmit to the USSR information relating to the national defense of the United States.

In light of the overwhelming evidence that Abel was a Soviet spy, his conviction was affirmed by the appellate court.

* * *

Having no success in the Second Circuit Court of Appeals, Abel then appealed the case to the US Supreme Court, where Abel would fare no better. Writing for the court in its 5-4 decision, Justice Felix Frankfurter—joined by Justices John Marshall Harlan, Charles E. Whittaker, and Potter Stewart—wrote that the overriding question in this case was whether seven items—seized by government officers without a search warrant—were properly admitted into evidence at Abel's trial for conspiracy to commit espionage.

Specifically, the court considered whether the Fourth and Fifth Amendments to the Constitution were violated by a search and the seizure of evidence without a search warrant after an alien suspected and officially accused of espionage has been taken into custody for deportation pursuant to an administrative immigration service warrant, but had not been arrested for the commission of a crime. There was also the question of whether the Fourth and Fifth Amendments to the Constitution were violated when the articles seized were unrelated to the immigration service warrant and, together with other articles obtained from such leads, were introduced as evidence in a prosecution for espionage.

The underlying basis of Abel's attack upon the admissibility of the challenged items of evidence concerned the motive of the government in its use of the administrative arrest. Abel alleged that the government resorted to a subterfuge, that the Immigration and Naturalization Service warrant was a pretense and sham, and that the government's true purpose in arresting Abel under this warrant was in order to (1) place Abel in custody so that pressure might be brought to bear upon him to confess his espionage and cooperate with the FBI, and (2) to permit the government to search through his belongings for evidence of his espionage to be used in a designed criminal prosecution against him. Abel contended that the government used the administrative warrant for illegitimate purposes and that the articles seized as a result should have been suppressed.

The Supreme Court agreed that the deliberate use by the government of an administrative warrant for the purpose of gathering evidence in a criminal case must be deterred by the courts, and that the preliminary stages of a criminal prosecution must be pursued in strict obedience to the safeguards and restrictions of the Constitution and laws of the United States.

But the Supreme Court concluded that a finding of bad faith was *not* shown on the record. The district court had found:

> [T]he evidence is persuasive that the action taken by the officials of the Immigration and Naturalization Service is found to have been in entire good faith. The testimony of Schoenenberger and Noto leaves no doubt that, while the first information that came to them concerning the [defendant]...was furnished by the FBI—which cannot be an unusual happening—the proceedings taken by the Department differed in no respect from what would have been done in the case of an individual concerning whom no such information was known to exist.

The district court further noted: "The defendant argues that the testimony establishes that the arrest was made under the direction and supervision of the FBI, but the evidence is to the contrary, and it is so found. No good reason has been suggested why these two branches of the Department of Justice should not cooperate, and that is the extent of the showing made on the part of the defendant." The court of appeals agreed.

In support of this finding, the Supreme Court pointed to the testimony of officer Noto that the interest of the INS in Abel was confined to Abel's illegal status in the country. In informing the INS about Abel's presence in the United States, the FBI did not indicate what action it wanted the INS to take, and Noto himself made the decision to arrest Abel and to commence deportation proceedings against him. The court pointed to the fact that the FBI made no request of Noto to search for evidence of espionage at the time of the arrest, and that it was "usual and mandatory" for the FBI and INS to work together in this way.

The Supreme Court did not ignore the evidence that the INS held off its arrest of the petitioner while the FBI solicited his cooperation, and that the FBI held itself ready to search Abel's room as soon as it was vacated. But the evidence of good faith to the contrary was found to be persuasive. The court admitted that the facts of the case revealed an opportunity for abuse of the administrative arrest, but to prohibit the cooperation between INS and FBI would be to unnecessarily restrict two branches of a single Department of Justice concerning enforcement of different areas of law under the common authority of the Attorney General.

The court reasoned:

The facts are that the FBI suspected petitioner both of espionage and illegal residence in the United States as an alien. That agency surely acted not only with propriety but in discharge of its duty in bringing petitioner's illegal status to the attention of the INS, particularly after it found itself unable to proceed with petitioner's prosecution for espionage. Only the INS is authorized to initiate deportation proceedings, and certainly the FBI is not to be required to remain mute regarding one they have reason to believe to be a deportable alien merely because he is also suspected of one of the gravest of crimes and the FBI entertains the hope that criminal proceedings may eventually be brought against him. The INS, just as certainly, would not have performed its responsibilities had it been deterred from instituting deportation proceedings solely because it became aware of petitioner through the FBI, and had knowledge that the FBI suspected petitioner of espionage.

The court continued:

The government has available two ways of dealing with a criminally suspect deportable alien. It would make no sense to say that branches of the Department of Justice may not cooperate in pursuing one course of action or the other once it is honestly decided what course is to be preferred. For the same reasons, this cooperation may properly extend to the extent and in the manner in which the FBI and INS cooperated in effecting petitioner's administrative arrest. Nor does it taint the administrative arrest that the FBI solicited petitioner's cooperation before it took place, stood by while it did, and searched the vacated room after the arrest. The FBI was not barred from continuing its investigation in the hope that it might result in a prosecution for espionage because the INS, in the discharge of its duties, had embarked upon an independent decision to initiate proceedings for deportation.

The court held that the administrative warrant was not employed as an instrument of criminal law enforcement to circumvent its legal restrictions, rather than as a bona fide preliminary step in a deportation proceeding.

Holding that Abel's arrest was valid, the court then considered the question whether the seven challenged items seized during searches that were a direct consequence of that arrest were properly admitted into evidence. The court explained that there can be no doubt that a search for weapons has as much justification here as it has in the case of an arrest for crime, where it has been recognized as proper. It was no less important for government officers, acting under established procedure to effect a deportation arrest rather than one for crime, to protect themselves and to insure that their prisoner retains no means by which to accomplish an escape.

The court concluded that government officers who make a deportation arrest have a right of incidental search analogous to the search permitted criminal law enforcement officers. The only items sought in this case were documents connected with Abel's status as an alien. These may well be considered as instruments or means for accomplishing his illegal status, and thus proper objects of search.

Two of the challenged items were seized during this search of Abel's property at his hotel room. The first was the forged New York birth certificate for "Martin Collins," one of the false identities which Abel assumed in order to keep his presence undetected. This item was seizable when found during a proper search, not only as a forged official document by which the petitioner sought to evade his obligation to register as an alien, but also as a document which the petitioner was using as an aid in the commission of espionage.

The other item seized in the course of the search of the petitioner's hotel room was a piece of graph paper containing a coded message. This was seized by Officer Schoenenberger as Abel, while packing his suitcase, was seeking to hide it in his sleeve. An arresting officer is free to take hold of articles which he sees the accused deliberately trying to hide. This power derives from the dangers that a weapon will be concealed or that relevant evidence will be destroyed. Once this piece of graph paper came into Schoenenberger's hands, it was not necessary for him to return it, because it was an instrumentality for the commission of espionage. This is so even though Schoenenberger was not only not looking for items connected with espionage, but could not properly have been searching for the purpose of finding such items.

The birth certificate for "Emil Goldfus" (who died in 1903), a certificate of vaccination for "Martin Collins," and a bank book for "Emil Goldfus" were seized not in the petitioner's hotel room, but in a more careful search at INS headquarters of the belongings the petitioner chose to take with him when arrested. This search was a proper one.

The admissibility of the hollowed-out pencil and the block of wood containing a "cipher pad" were founded upon an entirely different set of considerations. These two items were found by an agent of the FBI in the course of a search he undertook of Abel's hotel room, immediately after Abel paid his bill and vacated the room. They were found in the wastepaper basket, where Abel put them while packing his belongings and preparing to leave. No pretense was made that this search by the FBI was for any purpose other than to gather evidence of the crime of espionage. As such, however, it was entirely lawful, although undertaken without a warrant. This is so because, at the time of the search, Abel had vacated the room.

The hotel then had the exclusive right to its possession, and the hotel management freely gave its consent that the search be made. Nor was it unlawful to seize the entire contents of the wastepaper basket, even though some of its contents had no connection with crime. Abel had abandoned these articles, and the court held that there can be nothing unlawful in the government's appropriation of such abandoned property. The items were used means for the commission of espionage and were seizable as such. Since the two items were lawfully seized by the government in connection with an investigation of crime, they were admissible.

* * *

Justice William O. Douglas, joined by Justice Hugo Black, wrote the first dissenting opinion. He felt that the record plainly revealed that FBI agents were the moving force behind the arrest and search since they tracked Abel for a month and had plenty of time to obtain a search warrant from a magistrate instead of going to the INS to issue the arrest warrant.

According to Justice Douglas, the administrative warrant of arrest was chosen with care and calculation as the vehicle through which the arrest and search were to be made. Douglas noted that the FBI had an agreement with the INS that the warrant of arrest would not be served until Abel refused to "cooperate." The FBI agents went with agents of the INS to Abel's hotel room. It was the FBI agents who were first to enter Abel's room and interrogate him. When Abel refused to speak, they signaled agents of the INS, who had waited outside, to come in and make the arrest.

The search was made both by the FBI agents and by officers of the INS. And, when the petitioner was flown 1,000 miles to a special detention camp and held for three weeks, the agents of the FBI as well as the INS interrogated him. Thus, according to Douglas, the FBI used an administrative warrant to make an arrest for criminal investigation both in violation of § 242(a) of the Immigration and Nationality Act [Footnote 5] and in violation of the Bill of Rights.

Justice Douglas wrote:

> *The facts seem to me clearly to establish that the FBI agents wore the mask of INS to do what otherwise they could not have done.... How much more convenient it is for the police to find a way around those specific requirements of the Fourth Amendment! What a hindrance it is to work laboriously through constitutional procedures! How much easier to go to another official in the same department! The administrative officer can give a warrant good for unlimited search. No more showing of probable cause to a magistrate! No more limitations on what may be searched and when!*

The Fourth Amendment provision for "probable cause," he argued, requires that the warrant be drawn by a neutral and detached magistrate, not an overzealous law enforcement officer. In this case, the FBI worked exclusively through an administrative agency—the INS—to accomplish what the Fourth Amendment states can be done only by a judicial officer. In other words, a procedure designed to serve administrative ends—deportation—was cleverly adapted to serve criminal prosecution.

The second dissenting opinion was written by Justice Brennan, joined by Chief Justice Earl Warren and Justices Hugo L. Black and William O. Douglas.

Brennan contended that the arrest, while conducted under what is known as a warrant, was made totally without the intervention of an independent magistrate—it was made on the authorization of one administrative official to another. After Abel was taken into custody, there was no obligation on the administrative officials who arrested him to take him before any independent officer, sitting under the conditions of publicity that characterize our judicial institutions, and justify what had been done.

Instead, Abel was taken to a local administrative headquarters and then flown in a special aircraft to a special detention camp over 1,000 miles away and incarcerated in solitary confinement there. As far as the world knew, he had vanished. He was questioned daily at the place of incarceration for over three weeks. An executive procedure as to his deportability was conducted at the camp a few days later, but there was never any independent inquiry or judicial control over the circumstances of the arrest and the seizure until over five weeks after his arrest, when, at the detention camp, he was served with a bench warrant for his arrest on criminal charges, upon an indictment.

The Fourth Amendment imposes substantive standards for searches and seizures, and one of the important safeguards it establishes is a procedure, said Brennan, and central to this procedure is an independent control over the actions of officers conducting searches of private premises. Brennan concluded: "Indeed, the informed and deliberate determinations of magistrates empowered to issue warrants as to what searches and seizures are permissible under the Constitution are to be preferred over the hurried action of officers and others who may happen to make arrests."

EPILOGUE

In a strange twist of fate that only a novelist could concoct, four years and three months later Abel was back in the USSR, having been exchanged for U-2 aviator Francis Gary Powers, a CIA spy apprehended by the Soviet government after his plane crashed on May 1, 1960.

Powers had taken off from a military airbase in Peshawar, Pakistan, on a mission to photograph Russian military sites deep within Soviet airspace. His U-2 spy plane was capable of reaching altitudes over 70,000 feet, which was thought to be too high for Soviet surface-to-air missiles. One of the missiles exploded close enough to Powers's plane to send it careening toward the ground. He was unable to engage the plane's self-destruct switch before ejecting from the cockpit and parachuting to the ground.

It took several months of negotiating before James Donovan was sent to meet face to face with the second secretary of the Soviet Embassy, Ivan Schischkin, in East Germany. During that time, Donovan worked with the Department of Justice to set up the prisoner exchange. By agreeing to exchange Francis Power for Abel, the Soviets—reluctantly enough—had to admit who he was.

On the morning of February 10, 1962, the exchange took place at Glenicke Bridge, a riveted, dark-green steel structure spanning the Havel River near the East German town of Potsdam.

The "Bridge of Spies" where Abel was exchanged for Powers.

Allen Dulles, the head of the CIA at the time, commented that there were several implications of the exchange: "First of all, it meant the breakdown of Soviet pretentions that they had no responsibility for Abel, a position they took at the time of his arrest, trial, and conviction; and secondly, it opened up the possibility that the exchange of spy for spy might become a general practice.... I felt then and feel now that it was a fair exchange and that it was in our own interest to proceed with it under the particular circumstances of this rather unusual case. However, this has tended to create a precedent which may have some unfortunate consequences. The number of Soviet agents in the West, we may assume, greatly exceeds the number of Western agents they are detaining. If the idea of swapping agent for agent becomes the practice, the Soviet will be anxious to have a backlog of apprehended agents in their hands. Hence, they will be tempted, and will likely succumb to the temptation, to arrest casually visiting Westerners who have nothing whatsoever to do with intelligence."

The wooden-faced, sixty-two-year-old Abel walked into the fog of East Germany, along with the bygone era of espionage of crude shortwave radios, primitive microfilm, and hazy cipher pads.

* * *

In 1938—twenty years before the Abel case—a Soviet intelligence officer named Mikhail Gorin was working undercover in the United States, and he sent a pair of pants to the cleaners. He had carelessly failed to remove from the pockets a number of documents stolen from the Office of Naval Intelligence.

The dry cleaner removed the papers, and thus revealed one of the most serious cases of Soviet espionage on American soil. And all due to an extreme act of carelessness, much like Abel's revelation of his art studio to Häyhänen. Gorin was eventually returned to the Soviet Union, where he was likely executed for his misdeeds.

It has been said that there was no direct evidence indicating that Abel or his co-conspirators ever succeeded in transmitting any unlawful information to the Soviet Union. Abel was charged with having "conspired" to gather and transmit to the Soviet government secret information pertaining to the national defense of the United States, and the record was clear that Abel knew of the unlawful purpose of this conspiracy. The conspirators' lack of success did not alleviate the criminality of their activities.

In the Abel trial, Häyhänen testified under investigation by the prosecutor:

> Q. *Now, let me ask you this directly: What type of information were you seeking?*
>
> A. *Espionage information.*
>
> Q. *Would you describe that, what you mean by espionage information?*
>
> A. *By espionage information, I mean all information what you can look to get from newspapers or official way, by asking from,*

I suppose, legally from some office, and I mean by espionage information that kind of information what you have to get illegal way. That is, it is secret information for—

The court: *Concerning what? What kind of information?*

A. *Concerning national security or—*

The court: *What do you mean by that?*

A. *In this case United States of America.*

The court: *What do you mean by national security?*

A. *I mean it—that some military information or atomic secrets.*

Abel's attorney called this a "clearly rehearsed statement of a legal conclusion." But the courts reviewing the case did not agree. Häyhänen specifically testified that the purpose of the conspiracy was to obtain "military information or atomic secrets." His failure to elaborate concerning the information which the conspirators sought to acquire was explained in his prior response:

Q. *During this conversation or during the receipt of these oral instructions from [Vitali G.] Pavlov, did he give you any directions as to the type of information?*

A. *Yes, he did. He told that it depends what kind of illegal agents I will have, so it depends then what kind of information they can give, where they work or whom they have as friends and such and such things.*

Häyhänen had not been successful in his espionage activities, but he did describe a series of interactions with Abel—like the search for Sergeant Rhodes, whose relatives were thought to be working on military installations or atomic plants—which showed that Abel was aware of the purpose of the conspiracy. The jury must have been impressed by the elaborate precautions taken by the conspirators to keep their activities secret. Those who are intent upon gathering and transmitting only such information find it necessary to employ secret codes, microdots, hollowed-out coins, secret "drops," and the variety of other devices which Abel and his colleagues used.

Abel and his co-conspirators may or may not have succeeded with their plans, but an inference as to their purpose is properly drawn from the methods they employed. Proof of the methods they used would not alone be sufficient to sustain a conviction, but the courts held that a justifiable inference from the use of such methods, when considered together with the other evidence, was sufficient to justify the jury in finding that the object of the conspiracy in the present case was to gather and transmit to the USSR information detrimental to the national defense of the United States.

In a series of events presciently predicted by Abel's attorney James Donovan, Abel found himself back in the USSR. Abel was largely hailed as a hero on his return, and he received the acclaimed Order of Lenin in 1966. He died of lung cancer on November 15, 1971.

Spying, it seems, is a vicious and unpredictable two-way street, and one that can often be dangerous to cross.

Abel depicted on a Soviet postage stamp.